AFTER
GOD'S HEART

Bro. Larry + Melwyn,

May the Lord bless

y/n.

Bro. B

AFTER
GOD'S HEART
Becoming the Man God is Seeking

DERON J. BILES

Outskirts Press, Inc.
Denver, Colorado

Outskirts Press, Inc.
http://www.outskirtspress.com

ISBN: 978-1-4327-4836-4

Outskirts Press and the "OP" logo are trademarks belonging to Outskirts Press, Inc.

PRINTED IN THE UNITED STATES OF AMERICA

This book is dedicated to my four boys: Joshua, Timothy, Jonathan, and David whom I pray will be and I already see becoming men after God's Heart.

Table of Contents

Preface

On the occasion of King David's greatest sin, the Prophet Nathan came to visit him. Nathan told him a story that God used to change David's heart. The story was about a wicked and wealthy land owner who wanted to provide an impressive banquet for a visiting dignitary. However, instead of killing one of his many lambs, he stole the one little lamb of a poor man who lived nearby to provide for his guests. David was so incensed at the story of this wicked man that he exclaimed, "This man deserves to die." Nathan agreed. Then the Prophet pointed his finger at the greatest King in the known world at that time and declared, "YOU are that man!"

The Lord used the parable to bring conviction to David's heart and eventual restoration of fellowship. But, the description of the man and his little lamb in Nathan's story has long intrigued me. I've often told students in my classes that the picture that this story paints is very similar to the life that many pastors spend their entire ministries living. Think about the ingredients of the parable:

- A man who, by the world's standards, had very little. He only has ONE little Lamb – Not a BIG one but a LITTLE lamb!
- It came to him sacrificially. The text says he bought it. It came at a cost for him.
- He nourished that little lamb.
- His family shared in the costs as it grew up together with his them.
- It ate of his food.
- It lived among them and was family to him.

At one point or another in his life, David is every character in the story. At times, he was the bold prophet of God confronting the sinner (Goliath, Saul). At times, he was the man who had very little (cf. 1 Sam. 17:28; 18:18, 23; 24:14). Obviously, we know that in the story David represents the rich man who took from the poor man. One might even say there were times when David was like that little lamb that was taken (cf. 1 Sam. 18:2).

The parable may or may not be based on actual events, but it is a pretty good picture of the life of most pastors today. Now, to be sure, some have much bigger lambs; some even have more than one lamb. But, by and large, most pastors spend their entire ministries shepherding what might be described as little lambs.

But the parable is also true of the temptations that all men face. It's the struggle to be successful -- at all costs. It's the ability to see the faults in others and, yet, miss our own obvious failures. It's the temptation to try to get what we want when we want it and to do whatever we have to do to get it. This book is about the struggle that all men of faith face: the desire to be like God mixed with the selfishness to try do it our own way. Despite all that David wasn't, God still referred to him as "a man after God's own heart." Isn't that what you want? Wouldn't you want to be that man for your children? Your wife? Your church?

This book is not about trying harder for God. That won't do it. Instead, I want to examine the passages of Scripture that talk about what God was looking for and discovered in David. Each chapter will address keys that Scripture gives for becoming that kind of man. At the end of each chapter, there is a section entitled "Becoming the Man God is Seeking." These sections will focus on episodes in David's life in which he exemplified the lessons of that chapter. He didn't always do it right, and you won't either. But, with God's help and a holy hunger for God's best, God can make you and me more like men after His heart.

Introduction

There are no historical records of David outside of Scripture.[1] Thus, God's Word provides the parameters for our understanding of David. In His Word, God has provided the bases for His selection of David. Consider what God said of him: he was sought by God (1 Sam. 13:14); he was selected ("seen") by God as King (1 Sam. 16:1); he was His servant (Ps. 89:3, 20); he was chosen (Ps. 78:70; 89:3); he was appointed over God's people (1 Sam. 13:14); he was the recipient of God's promise (Ps. 89:3; 132:11; cf. 2 Sam. 7:8-17 and 1 Chron. 17:1-15); and he found favor with God (Acts 7:46). All of these convey the significance of Israel's greatest king. But, it is the first description of David by God that seems to most vividly portray his relationship with God; God described him as "a man after His own heart." Scripture twice records this description: once before David became King and the other long after (1 Sam. 13:14; Acts 13:22).

The Bible frequently described God's pursuit of David using the language of "one who was sought and found." As we will see in this study, David wasn't always seeking God, but God was always seeking him. What God found in David was a man who wanted what God wanted, who would serve Him with a pure heart, and who lived out God's purpose for his generation.

On four occasions, the Bible reveals what God sought and found in David. These passages, which serve as the general outline for this book, reveal essential truths for all men today who desire to be men after God's own heart, like David was. From 1 Samuel 13:14, we learn that David was a man known by his character; in Psalm 89:20-24, we see, exemplified in David, a man leading through service; in Acts 7:46, we discover how David was a man consumed by God's vision; and in Acts 13:22, we ascertain that David was a man pursuing God's mission. Those four characteristics: character, servant leadership, vision, and mission epitomize what God was looking for in a leader for His people.

As a result of this study in David's life, I hope that we, as men, learn two very valuable lessons of which all of us need to be reminded. First, God is still looking for men after His own heart. It will become abundantly clear that although David accomplished many wonderful things for the Lord, he was also a sinful man, as we are. One can't help but be struck by the alarming honesty with which the Bible presents the fabric of David's life. His faults aren't glossed over. They are there for all to see and learn. You can no longer use the excuse that because you're not perfect God can't use you. David wasn't perfect and look how God used him. God's search is ongoing.

The second lesson all of us as men should take from the story of David is that you and I can be men after God's heart. But, it's not about a formula. You won't find in this book an ABC pattern that you can just check off and presume to have accomplished what God is looking for in you. What David exemplifies most is a relationship with God. God also wants that with you. You may not face a Goliath, but you will face giants. You may not become king, but you will have opportunities of influence. You may not write songs, or play music, or be blessed with the same natural talents that David possessed, but God has gifted you in ways that are unique to you. God wants you to be a man after His own heart.

David wasn't perfect, and you won't be either. But, when David failed God, he always turned back to God. It's not that God doesn't desire faithfulness and holiness. Indeed, the lesson of David clearly establishes that. However, He is also a God of grace. The Bible says that if we will confess our sins that He is faithful and just to forgive us and to cleanse us from our unrighteousness (1 John 1:9). David may have been a great sinner; but, when you read his contrition, it seems that he was an equally great repenter. Don't use that as an excuse to do what you want and presume upon God's grace (cf. Rom. 6:1-2). But, when you sin, remember that He loves you and offers His forgiveness to you.

Don't just follow David. Develop of lifestyle of seeking the God who is seeking you. You are a man after God's hand. I want you to be a man after God's heart.

What Is A Man After God's Own Heart?

Throughout history, we see examples of people searching for someone. For some, it is a mate; for others, it is a companion. In some cases, people are searching for a hero, someone to believe in. Maybe you are searching for someone. Regardless, there is someone searching for you. Have you found who you are looking for?

Marcus Schrenker hasn't found him. Schrenker will forever be remembered as the failed financial manager who attempted to fake his own death to avoid his failed marriage, bad debts, and criminal charges. The man, once described as a "daredevil money manager," boarded his small plane, put it on autopilot, and made a distress call claiming that the plane's windshield had imploded, causing him to bleed. Then, Schrenker parachuted from his airplane and fled on a red motorcycle. The plane later crashed 200 miles away in a bayou in Santa Rosa County, Florida, near a residential area. Two days later, some US Marshals tracked him to a remote campground in northern Florida, apparently interrupting his suicide attempt.

A few weeks prior to his failed escape attempt, Schrenker was interviewed about his various financial and family difficulties and was quoted as saying, "I don't think that there is a good person left in this world." The irony is that here was a guy facing divorce, pretending to be someone he's not, twice filing for bankruptcy with huge unpaid debts, and planning to stage his own death while complaining that nobody else is good! But, he is not the only one looking for a good man.

On March 20, 1779, in Boston, Captain William Jones, of the United States Marine Corp, advertised for "a few good men" to enlist in the Corps for naval duty. The term seemed ideally suited for Marines, mainly because of the implication that "a few" good men would be enough. This term has survived for over 200 years and has been synonymous with U.S. Marines ever since. The Marines have found many good men but are still looking for a few more. Their search continues.

Twenty-four hundred years before Captain Jones, Jeremiah was instructed to "Run to and fro throughout the city [to see if he could] find a man … who executes judgment, who seeks the truth." If such a man could be found, God promised to save the city (Jer. 5:1). No such man was found, and the city was not saved.

Before Jeremiah, the Prophet Ezekiel recorded God's search for a man who would be able to "make a wall and stand in gap" on behalf of the city so that He would not have to destroy it. But, none was found (Ezek. 22:30).

Before the time of the prophets, the Psalmist cried

out to the Lord in Psalm 12:1, "Help, Lord, for the godly man ceases to be. He has disappeared from among the sons of men." His search proved futile.

More than 1000 years prior to that, Abraham was called upon by God to search the city for a few good men. One man was saved, but it was not enough to save the city. Throughout history, God's been looking for a good man. Most of the time, the search comes up empty. But, the Scripture records that in David, it seems, God found at least one.[2]

More space in the Bible is devoted to David than to any other person, including Jesus. His name occurs more than 1000 times in Scripture -- four times more than Abraham's. His life is covered in sixty-six chapters within four books of the Old Testament, and there are fifty-nine references to him in the New Testament. There are seventy-four Psalms specifically attributed to David:[3] seventy-three in the book of Psalms and one in 2 Samuel[4] are among the best-loved and most-often read passages in Scripture.[5] In addition, there are fifty Psalms that do not indicate the author. It is also possible that David was the author of some of them as well.

The stories of David's life are among the most well-known in the Bible. Children grow up learning of both David's greatest successes and worst failures.[6] In the Bible, he is described as loyal to God, attractive, ruddy (red-headed?), spirit-filled, God's Servant, and a man God found. In addition, David is depicted in the Bible as a son, brother, husband, father, shepherd, son-in-law to the King, friend, hunter, warrior, champion, musician, general, actor, king, prince, poet, worship leader, ladies' man, prophet, adulterer, murderer, outlaw, builder, administrator, and ancestor of Jesus Christ. Yet, of all the great things said about David, perhaps his best epitaph came ultimately from God who described him as "a man after God's heart."

Many are quick to mention David's failures, which are many and well-documented. First, the Bible records David's failures as a husband. David had a failed marriage with Michal, violated his marriage vows in his affair with Bathsheba, and failed to protect his concubines when he fled the city from Absalom. Second, the Bible records David's failures as a father. David's sinful actions, or inactions, negatively impacted at least six of his children (Tamar, Absalom, Amnon, Solomon, Adonijah, and the unnamed baby of Bathsheba). Third, the Bible records David's sin in the murder of Uriah. Fourth, the Bible records David's failure to repent for the entire period of Bathsheba's pregnancy. Fifth, the Bible records David's failure in the moving of the Ark of the Covenant and his anger at the Lord in His judgment. Sixth, the Bible records David's failure in leadership when he failed to deal with Joab's murder of Abner. Seventh, the Bible records David's failure in administration when he brought God's judgment on the nation by ignoring his advisors as well as God's Word in calling for a census. Others have pointed to:

- David's multiple wives;
- his inciting of Jonathan, Saul's son, to lie to his father;[7]
- his apparent mishandling of the situation with Mephibosheth and failure to address the deceit of Ziba;
- his half-truth to the Priest Ahimelech, eating of consecrated bread, and carelessness by not anticipating the actions of Doeg the Edomite which caused the death of Ahimelech and eighty-five priests at Nob;
- his angered response in the situation with Nabal;
- his apparent lack of faith in God by fleeing to King Achish twice (2 Sam. 21:10-15; 27:1-12);
- his willingness to fight with the Philistines against his own people, Israel;
- his apparent, and seemingly unnecessary, lie to king Achish about where he and his men had fought (2 Sam. 27:10), along with the atrocities he committed in those battles;
- his failure to plan for a smooth transition of power between his reign and that of his son's, Solomon, though God had given him clear instructions on his successor when David had even promised Bathsheba that Solomon would succeed him (1 Kings 1:30); and,
- the hit list of people to execute that he gave to his son, Solomon, to carry out, which included a

man named "Shimei" whom David promised he
would not punish (2 Sam. 19:23) as additional
illustrations of David's sinfulness.

In case you're counting, that's twenty-four. In fact,
there are more of David's sins delineated in Scripture
than those of any other character in the Bible. David
committed sins morally, familially, ethically, spiritually,
emotionally, and administratively. Bear in mind, these
failures range over a forty-year ministry but still represent significant moments of departure from God's clearly revealed will.

What's worse, several of David's sins affected many
other people. His family life was significantly affected.[8]
He was not the husband or father that he needed to
be. He was embarrassed when his sins became public
knowledge. He compromised his ability to speak with
moral authority against sins he had committed. Also,
because of his sins, lives were lost: Uriah and the child
born to David and Bathsheba died because of David's
sin with Bathsheba,[9] Uzzah died because of David's sin
in moving the Ark of the Covenant, eighty-five priests
died because of his sin with Ahimelech, seventy thousand men died because of his sin in commanding a census, many died because of the atrocities he committed
while fighting with the Philistines, and Shimei died because David went back on his word. The Bible is clear;
sin brings consequences. Oftentimes, the consequences
of our sin affect others as well.

Another Giant from Gath

After the events of David's mishandling of the situation with Ahimelech, David made another poor decision, followed by a strange response and an understandable result. In addition to receiving food from Ahimelech, the priest also gave to him the sword of Goliath (1 Sam. 21:9), which rightfully belonged to David anyway. David must have left Saul's presence in haste and did not bring a sword with him. He lied to Ahimelech to gain both his favor and the finest sword in all the land. Upon receiving the sword of the giant from Gath, David proceeded to make a decision that is difficult to understand. In an effort to flee from Saul, David sought asylum in the country of the giant he had killed and whose sword he was now bearing. David fled to the Philistines (10).

David now faced another giant from Gath. This time it was the giant of fear. This fear manifested itself in a decision that represented a lack of faith in God to protect him. So, David, instead, trusted in the enemy. This is reminiscent of the Israelites in the wilderness who, upon the first signs of struggle, were ready to appoint a new leader and go back to Egypt, the country from which God had supernaturally rescued them. David fled to the enemy, and his unusual behavior didn't stop there. When David, not surprisingly, was not well-received in Gath, he feared for his life again. This time, David was afraid that the Philistines would kill him. So, in desperation, David pretended to act insane. The Bible says that he let his saliva run down into his beard and began to scribble nonsensically on the doors. It was probably a sign of God's grace that the enemy king drove David away.

When David left Gath, he settled in the cave of Adullam (1 Sam.22:1). This must have been his home for some time, because three of David's psalms were apparently composed there (Ps. 34, 57, 142). While David was in the cave, word got out to his family. His brothers and "all his father's household" went to him (2). Along with them, they brought an army of debtors, along with many distressed and discontented people. It is possible that these represented people who felt disenchanted over the present leadership from King Saul. Or, this simply may be a case of David's attracting people who are like him.

Surprisingly, David later returned to Gath (1 Sam. 27:1). This time, sadly, David was granted a warmer reception by the enemy. David was afraid of Saul more than he was of the Philistines. He further compounded his poor decision with what might be described as "treason." David fought with the Philistines. Even worse, David was prepared to fight with the Philistines against Israel (1 Sam. 29:3-11). The Lord protected David from an act that could have kept him from the throne; and David is rejected from fighting with the enemy in the battle that Saul and Jonathan lost their lives. Can you imagine the Israelites seeing David fighting with the Philistines against them?

Failure Finds Few Friends

Often, David's failures were accentuated in his interpersonal relationships. While David was confrontational in battle, he was strikingly non-confrontational in dealing with people. This aversion to personal conflict is seen

Hypocrisy is a great De-motivator!

in his handling of, or rather, failure to address specific situations with Saul, Michal, Amnon, Absalom, Joab, Ziba, Shimei, Ahithophet, Sheba, and Adonijah. Several of these avoidances resulted in broken relationships (Michal, Absalom, Joab), while some even resulted in death (Amnon, Joab, Shimei, Adonijah). Often, David's unwillingness to confront others may have resulted from the guilt of his own sin. At least two of David's boys committed sins identical to those of their father (Amnon committed sexual sin and Absalom committed murder). It's no wonder David is hesitant to confront them; hypocrisy is a great demotivator!

David's hesitancy to confront led him to lie to Shimei and lose a relationship with Ahithophel, the grandfather of his wife, Bathsheba. Ahithophel was the father of Bathsheba's father Eliam (cf. 2 Sam. 11:3 and 23:34). He had been David's trusted counselor and sided with Absalom in his rebellion against David. I wonder what would have happened if David had sat down and counseled his former counselor.

There is a fine line between trusting in God to resolve crises in our lives and cowardly avoiding them in hopes that they will go away. More often than not, the consequences of not dealing with issues are far greater than the potential consequences of confronting them.

Be Careful to Whom You Listen

David didn't always follow good advice. The two greatest sins of David's life could have been avoided had he listened to the advice that was given him. The first came in the sad episode with Bathsheba. When David was tempted to sin against God by having an illicit affair with her, he called for a servant to make an inquiry regarding her. He wanted to know who she was and, if she was available. His assistant informed him well. David was told her name, her family background, her marriage status, and of her husband's loyalty to the king. The last three pieces of information seem intended by the servant to warn David against committing this sin against the Lord. Bathsheba was the daughter of Eliam. That may not seem significant, but it was. Not only was Eliam one of David's mightiest warriors, but Eliam was the son of one of David's chief advisors, Ahithophel (2 Sam. 23:34). Not only that, the king was informed that Bathsheba was married. In addition, not only was she married, but she was married to Uriah, another one of David's mighty men (2 Sam. 23:39). She was not some

unknown woman, she was well-known in the community. She was the daughter of one of David's elite military
forces and the granddaughter of one of David's advisors.
In addition, her husband also served as one of David's
special forces. Talk about a bad idea! The servant clearly recognized the sinfulness of the king's thoughts and
subtly warned him against them. But, David refused to
heed the advice of the servant.

Again, near the end of David's life, he failed to
heed good advice. One day, when the king had what he
thought was the great idea to number his people, his
military advisor, Joab, warned David that this was not
a good idea (2 Sam. 24:3). Joab, who certainly wasn't
renown for godliness, knew that David was pridefully
sinning against the Lord by numbering his people in
an effort to consider how great he had become. It was a
sin of arrogance, and, though David had not sought the
advice, he received appropriate counsel. He just didn't
follow the advice that he was given. Wisdom is knowing to whom to listen and heeding what might be God's
counsel through human mediators.

The Sounds of Silence

Finally, there are two very significant periods of
David's life where it appears that God was silent. Both
were occasions of David's sin: the first with Bathsheba
and the second in the taking of the census. Moreover,

both were approximately the same amount of time in length, around nine months.[10] Finally, in both cases, the period of silence was broken at God's initiative through the presence of a prophet with a message from God to David. How much time was wasted because David dwelt in unrepentance!

David addressed one of those periods of silence in Psalm 32. The psalm is about the virtues of being forgiven. However, in describing the long period of silence in his life, David highlighted another consequence of his sin when he said, "When I kept silent, my bones grew old through my groaning all the day long. For day and night Your hand was heavy upon me; My vitality was turned into the drought of summer" (32:3-4). David's sin brought separation between him and God, and it also brought physical pain. David described a wasting away of his body, literally, his bones. The word David used to express his groaning is the word used of a lion roaring. The guilt of his unconfessed sin brought physical pain to such extent that David felt the very life being drained from him. Sin always has consequences.

To be sure, David committed great failures. Aren't you glad someone isn't following you around recording all of your failures? Some of David's failures seem understandable given the circumstances he faced. Several of them occurred when he was fleeing for his life from King Saul. Others are reactions to circumstances. You and I must guard ourselves against sinful reactions to what happens to us.

One of the most appealing aspects of the Bible is its honesty. God's Word doesn't try to sugarcoat the failures of His people. That's one of the many reasons why we know we can trust Scripture. In fact, God tells us in His Word that we are all sinful before Him. There has never been anyone, other than Christ, who has always gotten it right. David was no exception.

The Bible never records that David always did right. Yet, both before his reign began and long after his life was completed, the Bible declared him to be a man after God's heart. Strangely, believers today can find comfort in that because "all have sinned and come short of the glory of God." Thus, becoming the man God seeks should be the goal that all men pursue. God's Word provides the prescription.

God's First Choice

God's initial pronouncement of David as a man after His heart came upon the occasion of Saul's first great failure. The Philistines, Israel's perennial enemy were threatening to attack and Saul and his forces were growing anxious. The enemy gathered in force: 30,000 chariots (each with two-to-three archers aboard), 6000 horsemen, and an army "like the sand on the seashore in abundance" (1 Sam. 13:5). As the enemy set up camp nearby, Saul's men grew faint and began to scatter. Some ran away; others hid in caves, thickets, cliffs, cellars, and pits. Even those who remained with the king trembled in fear. But, Samuel wasn't there.

For seven days, Saul waited for the Prophet. The King knew he needed to seek the blessing of the Lord through the intercessory work of the man of God. But, how long could he wait? The enemy was moving in, and his forces were moving out. He wanted God's blessing, but he didn't want to wait. He felt like he couldn't wait.

When the appointed time for the prophet was past, Saul took matters into his own hands. He sought God's favor while violating His will. Perhaps he felt justified. After all, hadn't he waited long enough? Besides, offering sacrifices to God was an act of worship even if it wasn't the way God instructed. At least, he sought God, right?

1 Samuel 13:10 is one of those really gut-wrenching verses in Scripture. If it weren't that we can so easily indentify with the feeling, it would be funny. The Bible says that as soon as Saul finished offering a sacrifice to the Lord, Samuel arrived. That is, the moment he finished trying it his own way, God showed up.

"What have you done, Saul?" The Prophet inquired.

"Well," the King replied, "I saw that the people were scattering from me, and that you did not come within the appointed days, and that the Philistines were assembling in Michmash, ... and I have not asked the favor of the Lord...." Saul's got a lot of excuses.

So, what'd you do?

Well, "I forced myself and offered the burnt offering," he replied.

Samuel's apparent delay became a test of faith for King Saul. Would he trust in God's time? Saul failed the test. He feared losing his armies more than he trusted in God. He trusted in the ritual of sacrifice more than the God who would bless it.

His refusal to wait upon the Lord brought the rebuke of the Prophet and the loss of a dynasty. Samuel's pronouncement revealed that what could have been a great dynasty through Saul and his offspring was forfeited because of his failure to keep the command of the Lord. Although the judgment delivered through Samuel marked the end of Saul's dynasty, it was God's grace that allowed him to continue to reign.

Saul would later compound this sin, by refusing to follow God's instructions. Like the episode above, Saul's second great failure revolved around his desire to sacrifice to God as he chose. Though he was given clear instructions in battle to spare no one and take nothing, Saul violated both commands. When he was confronted by Samuel, he protested that it was only his intention to offer what he kept for himself as a sacrifice to God. Samuel was not impressed, and God was not pleased (1 Samuel 15). The Prophet's rebuke of Saul seems to build on the earlier sin as Samuel pronounced, "You have rejected the word of the Lord, He has also rejected you from being king" (15:23).

The context is clear; Saul was not doomed from the start. Had he repented, God would have forgiven him. Had he been obedient, God would have blessed his kingdom and dynasty. Yet, even as Eli's house (dynasty) was similarly rejected (1 Sam. 2:30-36) for their unfaithfulness, so also was Saul's. Like a period before the end of the sentence, Samuel pronounced the end for Saul. His reign was not over, but his dynasty would not last beyond himself. Though God had chosen Saul, Saul had not chosen God.

Some have pointed to Saul's two statements of acknowledgement of his sin to Samuel as repentance (1 Samuel 15:24, 30). However, note that even in the acknowledgement of his sin, Saul doesn't turn to God. He turned to the Prophet to make it right with God for him. Saul always wanted the things of God his own way.

These two sins of Saul represent a heart of unfaithfulness to God. They resulted in God's removal of his dynasty and his rejection of Saul as king. In many ways they distinguish Saul's reign. It's the story of what could have been.

The Man God Was Looking For

It's not entirely clear when the events of 1 Samuel 13 took place in Saul's reign; however, some scholars point to the reference in 13:1 as a time stamp for these events.[11] The first part of the verse indicates Saul age

when he began to reign.[12] The second half of the verse
seems to be stipulating that in his second year, the events
of Chapter 13 took place. If that is the case, very early in
Saul's reign, which would last a total of forty years,[13] the
Lord had already found a man who would follow him
and had already appointed him.

What's interesting here is that God had chosen and
appointed David even before the future King was born.[14]
Note that in 1 Sam 13:14, David was not even named.
It was not until years later before steps were taken to secure Saul's successor. Jeremiah had a similar experience.
When God called him to be a prophet He declared,
"Before I formed you in the womb I knew you, and before you were born I consecrated you; I have appointed
you ..." (Jer. 1:5). Now, though only Saul and Samuel
knew it and though he wasn't even born yet, God had
already found Saul's successor.

Then, Saul's second great sin marks the beginning of
the end of his reign. God sent Samuel to Jesse's house
to find a successor for Saul. In 1 Samuel 16:12, God
said, "Arise, anoint [David] for this is he." Interestingly,
David's anointing was kept secret for a considerable
amount of time before God's was ready to carry out His
will in David's life. God didn't unfold His plan all at
once. Instead, there was a process that began in David's
youth while God was arranging the circumstances in
which David would reign over His people.

Are you waiting on God's time in your life? Maybe
God has revealed something that He is going to do in

your life that He has not yet done. Peter said, "The Lord is not slow about His promise as some count slowness, but is patient towards you not wishing for any to perish" (2 Peter 3:9). The truth is, you and I can't see the big picture. It might be that you are ready. Jack Graham said it well, "You can't hurry holiness."[15] God may still be working in you to prepare you for His will. It might be that the conditions are not right. You don't want to be in the right place at the wrong time. Always remember, God is faithful to His Word. Paul said that the One who calls you is faithful and He will bring His Word to pass (1 Thess. 5:24). If you want to be God's choice, you have to wait on God's time.

God's selection of David wasn't dependent upon Samuel; he got it wrong. Samuel was looking for a king who looked like Saul. He was ready to anoint Jesse's oldest and most impressive looking boy, but Eliab wasn't God's choice. God's choice for the next King, wasn't dependent on David's family, either. They, too, got it wrong. Jesse was so certain that the new king would be chosen among his first seven boys, he didn't even bring David before the Prophet who had called for all Jesse's sons to be presented before him. David is seen as an afterthought by his own father in the story. God's work in David's life was not dependent upon David's skill, even though he was a man of great skill. God pointed out to the Prophet, "Don't look at the outward appearance," God looks at the heart. God's will for David did not depend on David's charisma or good looks, despite his obvious charm and attractive description. It wasn't even dependent on the circumstances being right for David to step in as King. The Bible says that this was a time when everyone did what was right in his or her own eyes. Instead, David's selection depended completely on God.

Samuel declared that "The Lord has sought for Himself a man after His own heart." This was the same promise that God made through the Prophet, Jeremiah. He said, "I will give you shepherds after My own heart" (Jer. 3:15). It is God's divine providence both to choose and to remove. David would later affirm God's prerogative to choose declaring, "For the sake of Your word, and according to Your own heart, You have done all this greatness" (2 Sam. 7:21).

The Prophet announced, in 1 Samuel 13:13-14, the finality of God's declaration. Saul had not kept the command of the Lord which He commanded him. So, the Lord appointed that the one He had sought for Himself be made King because Saul did not keep what was commanded of him. Samuel wanted to be very clear; the Lord who commanded Saul to be King also commanded him to be removed and, now, commanded another to be King because Saul did not do as he was commanded. Thus, by not keeping the Lord's command with regards to the sacrifice, Saul had forfeited his position as King.

Later, Saul would be rejected by God again. So, in Saul's first rejection what was lost was a lasting Kingdom; in the second rejection, it was a personal rejection of

Saul. David's first anointment is mentioned as part of the consequences of Saul's disobedience.

In the end, the Bible records the demise of King Saul: "But he did not inquire of the Lord; therefore He killed him, and turned the kingdom over to David the son of Jesse" (1 Chron. 10:14). Thus, the Chronicler concludes that God removed Saul and handed the Kingdom over to David.

The Man Who Would Be the Man After God's Heart

Some have tried to water-down the impact of the Bible's description of David as a man after God's heart by advocating that this phrase only means "of his own choosing."[16] The agenda behind most such efforts is to suggest that somehow David wasn't the man the Bible describes him to be. Proponents of this theory point to the use of the identical phrase in 1 Samuel 14:7 and Psalm 20:4 as evidence. It must be noted that while the occurrence of this phrase in Psalm 20:4 seems to support the interpretation as "of his choosing," in 1 Samuel 14:7, a different preposition is used, which occurs seventeen times in the Old Testament and is better translated "in your heart" and not "according to your heart." However, these agenda-driven, skeptical scholars miss similar uses of this phrase in Jeremiah 3:15, which clearly refers to one's heart (character) being like unto God's;

in Deuteronomy 20:8, which describes the negative attributes of one's heart, that would adversely affect those around him; in 2 Samuel 17:10, which describes one's heart like the heart of a lion; in Jeremiah 48:41; 49:22, which describes the pain of a woman in labor; in Ezekiel 28:2, 6, where the King of Tyre is reminded that he is a man and NOT a god "though you say of yourself that you have a heart like that of a god;" and, perhaps, most significantly in 1 Kings 11:4; 15:3, which states that the hearts of Solomon and Abijam were not "according to the heart of David" which was "wholly devoted to the Lord."

It is similarly in vogue today to question the biblical texts' representation of David. Some scholars today, even accuse the Chronicler of "whitewashing" the account of David's life,[17] glossing over his failures so as to make him seem better than he was. But, consider all who must be wrong if David was NOT a man after God's heart. First, Samuel, who declared the prophecy of God in 1 Samuel 13:14, would have to been wrong for making a false prophecy. Second, Paul was wrong for restating that prophecy of Samuel in Acts 13:22 and declaring it to have been true in David. Third, Luke would have to have been wrong for recording it. Fourth, the Chronicler would have to have been wrong for "whitewashing" the life of David and focusing on the impact of David on every subsequent King of Judah. Fifth, the Holy Spirit would have to have been wrong for inspiring both a prophecy and fulfillment. The impact of the Holy Spirit's inspiration is even seen in the clear juxtaposition of Saul and David in the literature of the Old Testament. Sixth, if David was not a man after God's own heart, then God was wrong for choosing unwisely after the Prophet declared that God would find such a man (cf. 1 Kings 11:34). Seventh, Jesus would have to have been wrong for allowing Himself to be called the Son of David. Eighth, David would have to be considered wrong in Psalm 4:3, when he declared that God set him apart as one who is godly. Ninth, the Psalmist (Ethan) would have to be wrong who declared David to be the one who was chosen by God. Finally, if David was not a man after God's own heart, history has been wrong for highlighting David's impact on the nation of Judah and the faith of Christians. David's impact has been seen noted in such descriptions as "the City of David," "the throne of David," and "the House of David."

Indeed, to deny what God's Word clearly declares is to deny its truth and call into question its reliability at any point. It is also worth noting the presence of the Spirit of the Lord upon David's at his anointing. Additionally, David's own plea for God to "create in me a clean heart, O God, and renew a steadfast spirit within me" (Ps. 51:10) is an effort to retrieve that which God said he once had – a heart that pleased God.

It is clear that the Chronicler wrote with a different purpose than the writers of the books of Samuel and Kings. However, he wrote using frequent references to the earlier works and with the expectation that the readers were already familiar with them. Rather, the Chronicler's purpose appears to be "to show the returned remnant the vitality of hope they ought to have in the ultimate fulfillment of the Davidic Covenant."[18]

Thus, the central question of the life of David and his impact on the nation of Judah is not "How can one be more like David?" but, rather, "How can one have a heart like that of God which was exemplified in David?" That is the impact of the life of David. It should also be the motivation of men in the church today. The church has witnessed the waning impact of men in recent years. Statistics from every major denomination are consistent, and consistently bad. The role of men in the church is declining precipitously.[19] In fact, a survey conducted by George Barna revealed:

- In most churches today, women make up sixty per cent of the congregation, and there are between eleven million and thirteen million more "born again" women than "born again" men in the United States
- women are 100 percent more likely to be involved in discipleship than men
- women are fifty-seven percent more likely to participate in a small Bible study or prayer group than men
- women are forty-six percent more likely to disciple others in faith than men

- women are thirty-three percent more likely to volunteer their time and help to church than are men
- women are twenty-nine percent more likely than men to read the Bible
- women are twenty-nine percent more likely than men to share faith with others
- women are twenty-three percent more likely to donate to a church than men
- women are sixteen percent more likely than men to pray.[20]

Perhaps the most critical issue facing the church today is the need to recapture the impact of men in our ministry. D. L. Moody once said, "The world has yet to see what the Lord could do with one man, fully committed to Him." Wouldn't it be great if we could witness a day when that statement was no longer true? Moody's desire was to be that man. Is it yours?

David was a man after God's heart. That sounds impressive. Our tendency is to presume that becoming a man after God's heart is a standard which we are incapable of reaching. But, wouldn't that also be God's desire for you and me? What would it mean for you to be a man after God's Heart? Throughout history, God has been looking for a man. He's still looking. So, before they find us off hiding somewhere and mumbling to ourselves about what we are not, let's examine what it would take to be what God seeks.

Becoming the Man God Is Seeking

When we first meet David in Scripture, he is doing what he was instructed to do, tending sheep. But, the Lord knew, and the reader soon learns, that God was using that time as training in David's life. The lions and bears he would fend off today would be used as preparation for much more ferocious enemies tomorrow.

Even after David was first anointed king (1 Sam. 16:1-13), the next time we see David in the text, he is tending sheep (19). He would later serve King Saul faithfully as a demon-chasing musician, a giant-chasing warrior, a son-in-law, and a personal body guard. It would be as much as ten years after he was anointed before David would ever rule as king.

Do you imagine that David ever grew impatient on God's timing? Most of us know that David was a master musician and song writer. But, have you ever considered the circumstances behind the songs David wrote? Occasionally, the headings of the Psalms give the reader an indication of the circumstances in the author's life that gave rise to the music. They are reflections of the background behind the music. There are fourteen Psalms of David that include a historical preface (Pss. 3, 7, 18, 30, 34, 51, 52, 54, 56, 57, 59, 60, 63, and 142), and at least nine of them were written before David became king. You will read in those songs prayers of trust, prayers for security, prayers for deliverance, prayers of praise, prayers of thanksgiving, prayers of humility, and, even, prayers of hope. But, you will look in vain to find prayers of impatience.

God may have you "in the field" preparing for what He has for you next. While you are there, do your job well. Learn all that God wants you to learn. Prepare all you can. Learn to kill lions and bears. And, wait for God's perfect time. He won't be late. When His time is right and He knows you are ready, God will do in your life what only God can do.

Your alternative is to do it your own way. Saul tried that. We'll see later how that worked for him. For now, consider what Scripture says to you about becoming the man God seeks. To become who God seeks, you have to become who God wants. You to be ready for when God wants to use you.

A Man After God's Heart Is Not A Self-made Man

2

Our country has just come through the Presidential election process. The system is based upon the people's right to choose their leaders. The system is by no means perfect but maintains the privilege and responsibility of the citizens to participate in the selection of their leaders. The obvious deficiency of representative government is that flawed and ill-informed people oftentimes choose leaders who are flawed and ill-equipped to lead.

This was not the case with Israel. Their leaders were initially chosen by God, and their successors were intended to be taken from their progeny. The idea of the monarchy wasn't God's idea; it came from Israel. 1 Samuel 8:6-7 records the account when Israel insists that Samuel appoint for them a King. The text says, "Samuel was displeased when they asked for a king to judge them. The text is not clear if Samuel is displeased because he felt personally rejected, or if he felt like his family was being rejected from serving as a prophet of God and leader of the people after him.

Samuel prayed to the LORD, however, who

instructed the Prophet to grant the people's every request. He told Samuel, "It is not you they reject; they are rejecting me as their king." Instead, the people told the Prophet, "There shall be a king over us, that we also may be like all the nations, that our king may judge us and go out before us and fight our battles" (1 Sam. 8:19-20). Thus, while King David proved to be a man after God's heart, the actual institution of the monarchy in Israel represented leadership after Israel's heart, and not God's.

While Samuel, the ruling judge, took their request as a personal rejection of his leadership, the Lord ultimately explained that the people were not rejecting Samuel or even the institution of Judges; they were rejecting Him. But, the monarchy never proved to be what the people had hoped. In fact, the histories of both Israel and Judah reveal that smooth transitions of power were rare. The once-united nation quickly divided, and the histories of both nations were marked by disobedience and Divine judgment.

The northern kingdom of Israel had twenty monarchs, none of whom were declared by God to be good. Israel existed in the divided kingdom for approximately 210 years. The longest reigning king (Jeroboam II, cf. 2 Kings 14:23) lasted forty-one years, while the shortest (Zimri, cf. 1 Kings 16:15) reigned for only seven days! During that time, Israel had nine ruling dynasties with at least seven ending with assassinations. One of Israel's kings committed suicide (Zimri), and another was "stricken by God" (Jeroboam), and one was taken captive to Assyria (Hoshea).

The southern kingdom of Judah fared slightly better. It lasted for approximately 345 years. During that time, there were twenty monarchs in Judah, and eight of them were evaluated by God as good. The longest reigning king of Judah (Manasseh) reigned for fifty-five years, while two (Jehoahaz and Jehiachin) tied for the shortest reigns with three months. During that time, Judah saw basically only one ruling dynasty (with a brief interlude in story of a non-Davidic ruler in Athaliah) with at least five assassinations. Five were taken captive by foreign countries (Amaziah, Jehoahaz, Jehoiakim, Jehoiachin, Zedekiah), and two were stricken by God (Asa, Ahaz). The Scripture declared of Judah, "Also Judah did not keep the commandments of the Lord their God, but walked in the customs which Israel had introduced" (2 Kings 17:19 cf. 1 Kings 14:22).

Thus, the monarchy was not what God desired nor what Israel intended. It was God's intention that He would be their king. Yet, even in a system not intended by God, the selection of David as King stands out as unique and not based on the same criteria that Israel used. The Lord declared, "'I have found David the son of Jesse, a man after My own heart, who will do all My will'" (Acts 13:22).

The selection of David was a heart matter. After all, as God reminded Samuel, "For the Lord does not see as man sees; for man looks at the outward appearance, but the LORD looks at the heart" (1 Sam. 16:7). In David, God found a man who was like the heart of God.

The Bible suggests three things about the selection of David that ought to be paramount in the selection of any of God's leaders: God chose David, God raised David up, and God equipped David for the task.

God Will Choose for Himself

One of the most striking aspects of David's selection is the presence of God's hand in the process. It is true that the Bible indicates that God directed Samuel to Saul as Israel's first king, but that was only because the people had rejected God as their king. But, in the selection of David, God takes an even greater role. He directed the Prophet to the home where a new king would be found, changed Samuel's mind when he became distracted by the outward appearances of those who were not chosen, and announced the character of the man for whom He was searching before David's name was even mentioned in the text.

Highlighted in the story is the sovereignty of God. He is free to choose whomever He desires. Four centuries later, Jeremiah would be taught a similar lesson. The Lord sent the Prophet to a Potter's house. Jeremiah watched as the Potter molded the clay however he chose. God reminded his servant, "O house of Israel, can I not do with you as this potter? ... Look, as the clay *is* in the potter's hand, so *are* you in My hand, O house of Israel" (Jer. 18:6).

Paul would later reflect on those same words and add, "Will the thing formed say to him who formed *it,* 'Why have you made me like this?' Does not the potter have power over the clay from the same lump to make one vessel for honor and another for dishonor?" (Rom. 9:20-21).

The lesson of the text is that God has the right to determine the direction for our lives. The Psalmist declared, "My times are in Your hand" (Ps. 31:15). Indeed, the Father controls our very lives and calls whomever He chooses to be His servants. And, the work to which He calls us is for His honor and glory (Cf. Phil. 2:13). We don't call ourselves and, ultimately, can't equip ourselves for His service. Paul reminded us that the One who called us in faithful, and He will accomplish His purposes in and through us (1 Thess. 5:24).

We're all tired of the fall-out of those who have forsaken their calling. Some of those may have simply fallen victim to the temptation of the enemy. Others of them may have failed because they were never God-called. They may have been self-called, Momma or Daddy-called, or someone else-called. But, only God has the right to call men into His service. You and I have the right to refuse His calling (that is the risk God took in allowing us freedom of choice), but we don't have the right to call ourselves. The most important issue for a minister, next to his salvation, is his calling from God.

Samuel declared with confidence in 1 Samuel 13:14, "God will raise up a man." In other words, God is going to see that His work is done. When the time came for Samuel to anoint a new king, the Lord sent the Prophet to the home of Jesse. Not knowing whom God had chosen, Samuel began to interview Jesse's sons beginning with the oldest. When the oldest first appeared, Samuel was sure that he had to be the one. The reason: he looked like Saul. He was big, strong, and good-looking. He looked the part. But, the Lord had to remind Samuel that He does not base His decisions on what's on the outside but what is on the inside. Looks can be deceiving.

Samuel interviewed seven of Jesse's sons and did not find the man for whom God was looking. "Are all the young men here?" Samuel asked. "No," Jesse told him. "There remains yet the youngest, and there he is, keeping the sheep." When Samuel saw David, the Lord told him to "arise, anoint him; for this is the one" (1 Sam. 16:11-12).

Interestingly, when David is first introduced in the text, it is his outward appearance that is accentuated. He was described as ruddy (red), with bright eyes (a Hebrew phrase meaning "beautiful"), and good look-ing. Now, David often has the reputation of being short. Actually, the Bible never says that David was short -- just that he was shorter than Saul and shorter than Goliath. Nevertheless, when you put all of David's physical descriptions together, you get a composite picture of a short, cute, red-head. Quite a contrast to man who currently resided on the throne who looked the part yet didn't live it!

But, God sees what's on the inside. You and I can't hide it from Him. He knows. Adam tried to hide. Saul tried to hide. Elijah tried to hide. But, as the Lord declared, "Can a man hide in secret without my seeing him? ... Do I not fill both heaven and earth?" (Jer. 23:24).

God will choose for Himself a man to do the work He desires. God chose David. God has also chosen you.

The One God Chooses, He will Raise Up

God doesn't order anything He can't pay for. Luke recorded that when the Lord removed Saul from being king, "He raised up David as king" (Acts 13:22). Even more, God also "raised up" Jesus as Savior through David's offspring. Thus, the humble shepherd boy became the progenitor of the Messiah because God raised him up.

Those whom God has chosen, He will also call. All of us as believers have a special role that God has prepared for us in His Kingdom. It's easy to get caught up in where we would like to serve Him. But, doesn't that seem backwards? It's not our place to try to manipulate a place of service or pull the right strings to "get in" to the best positions. God will provide the place when He is ready.

Many ministers are enticed by the allure of something bigger and better: a bigger church, a higher salary, more prominence. And, the more they dream about something else, the less they are satisfied with where God has them now. But, Luke reminds us that God is faithful to His promise. He knows where you live. God will raise you up.

That was the same promise that God made to Moses. God assured him that He would raise up for Israel a Prophet, like Moses. God always has a plan. You and I don't get to choose our place in God's plan, but isn't it an act of grace that He allows us even to have a part in it?

It may not happen in the time that you would like. It didn't for David. The Bible records that God had chosen David in 1 Samuel 13. David was anointed as King in 1 Samuel 16. However, even after David was anointed king, he didn't begin serving as king. After David was anointed, but before he began to reign, he served the one who was king as a servant,[21] fought the giant, was persecuted by the king, fled the capital city from the king, wandered in the wilderness and in caves, spared the life of the king he would replace - twice (even though killing him would have hastened his own ascension to the throne), faced the death of his mentor (Samuel), allied with his enemies, fought in battles, and began to raise a family. Even when Saul died, knowing it was about to be his time to reign as king, David didn't rejoice. He knew God's time was right.

God's time is right for you, too. God may not have promised you an earthly kingdom, but His plan for you is best. Trust His will and His time.

I've had the privilege of working with a number of pastor search committees. My advice to them is always the same. "You're looking for God's man in God's time." Obviously, the wrong man at the right time is wrong, but the right man at the wrong time is also wrong!

It's the same in our lives. You and I are looking for God's plan in God's time. In Habakkuk 2, God gave the Prophet a vision. He told him to write it down clearly so all the people could understand it. Then God said, "The vision is yet for an appointed time; but at the end it will speak, and it will not lie. Though it tarries, wait for it; because it will surely come, it will not tarry" (Hab. 2:3).

My friend, God IS at work in your life (cf. Phil. 2:13). But, His plan has a time table. Don't try to manipulate God's plan before His time ... it's too soon! And, don't procrastinate when God reveals His will ... it may be too late!

The Scripture declares, "The eyes of the Lord move to and fro throughout the earth that He may strongly support those whose hearts are completely His" (1 Chron. 16:9). When God's time is right, He will raise you up. And, when God raises you up, you're in the right place at the right time.

The One God Raises Up, He will Equip

Henry Blackaby says that God works in men's lives through four steps. First, God chooses a man. Second God calls the man. Third, God prepares the man. Finally, God uses the man.[22] God's not going to call you to a task for which He has not or will not equip you. The Apostle Paul reminded the Church in Philippi that it was God who called them and He would complete the work He began *in* them, and that the God who was at work in them would accomplish His purposes *through* them (Phil. 1:6; 2:13).

The Psalmist reminded us that when God chose David, He also promised to strengthen and protect him. He declared:

Then You spoke in a vision to Your holy one, And said: "I have given help to *one who is* mighty; I have exalted one chosen from the people. I have found My servant David; With My holy oil I have anointed him, with whom My hand shall be established; Also My arm shall strengthen him. The enemy shall not outwit him, Nor the son of wickedness afflict him. I will beat down his foes before his face, and plague those who hate him. But My faithfulness and My mercy *shall be* with him, And in My name his horn shall be exalted (Ps. 89:19-24).

Note the prominence of the personal pronouns in this passage: "I" have given; "I" have exalted; "I" have found; "I" have anointed; "I" will beat down his foes; "My" servant David; "My" holy oil; "My" hand; "My" arm; "My" faithfulness; "My" mercy; "My" name. Did you catch His point? God will prepare and take care of His chosen ones. The enemy won't outwit him, afflict him, or defeat him. How God will work doesn't really matter. God doesn't always give us all the how's. Probably because we couldn't understand it anyway (cf. Is. 55:8-9; John 3:12). But, maybe even more because He wants us to trust Him. God told Jeremiah at his calling to go wherever God sent him and say whatever God told him to say (Jer. 1:7). Our job isn't to understand how God is going to do His part -- just to do ours. But, rest assured, if God's called you, He will equip you.

So, what do you do in the meantime? Keep being faithful where you are.[23] Stay where you are until God moves you. His timing is right and His plan for you is good. God will raise up a man. The question is when God calls, will you be ready?

Becoming the Man God Is Seeking

Does your life demonstrate evidence that God is making a difference in you? Right before David was officially made king, there was an episode in his life that challenged his faith in God. The circumstances came about as a result of David's sin in turning to the Philistines instead of God. But, when desperation set in, David remembered his ultimate source of strength.

David and his men were fighting alongside of the

Philistines. In fact, they were volunteering to fight against Israel. It could have been considered an act of treason. More importantly, it was a lack of faith. David was fleeing from Saul and turned to the Philistines instead of God. They lived with the enemy for a year and four months (1 Sam. 27:7).

Maybe you can relate. Have you spent too much time living in enemy territory? Perhaps, you have allowed sin to remain in your life. Like David, you may have wasted time lingering in the camp of the adversary instead of turning to God in faith. In David's case, his lack of faith had severe consequences. Though David volunteered to fight for the wrong team, God protected them. Later, when David and his men returned to the place among the Philistines where they had been living in Ziklag, they found that another foe had attacked. While they were offering their services to fight against God's people, the Amalekites raided their camp, burned it with fire, stole their possessions, and took their families hostage (1 Sam. 30:1-2). When David and his men discovered what had happened, they wept "until they had no more power to weep" (30:4). Worse, David's men blamed him. Talk of stoning him began to circulate in the camp as the people's anger turned to bitterness against their leader.

At this point, David was a very lonely man. In trying to protect his family, he put them in danger. He had nowhere to turn. He couldn't turn to his job, because they had rejected him. Even the enemy didn't want

David to fight with them. One could understand why the Philistines distrusted David. He had spent much of his life defeating them. As men, we often turn to our jobs for solace. When all else fails, at least, we have our work. Fighting had been David's life. Now, he couldn't even do that. He has been rejected. He was fired.

Secondly, David couldn't turn to his co-workers; they were the ones talking about stoning him. Many of those who served with David were his family and friends (1 Sam. 22:2). Now, in their grief, they turned against him. The very people who had come to David because of their discontentment, now turned against him when even greater trials emerged.

Third, David couldn't go home, he no longer has one. The Amalekites burned it. There's nothing like home. It doesn't matter if you live in a small apartment or a sprawling mansion, there's nothing like

Never forget, you never have nowhere to turn!

home. It is a place where a man can relax and be himself. It's a place where you can put aside the stress of the day and refresh. But, David's home was gone.

Fourth, David couldn't turn to his family, they had been taken. Samuel informs us that even David's wives were among the captives (30:5). In addition to having to deal with being rejected at work, blamed by his co-workers, and suffering the loss of their possessions, David had potentially lost his family. Where do you turn when you have nowhere else to turn? David "strengthened himself in the Lord, his God" (30:6). He found strength in God.

Hopefully, you and I don't only turn to God in desperation. God never intended our faith to just be a safety net. God wants a relationship with you. He wants to be your guide every day, not just when you are in trouble. But, never forget, you never have nowhere to turn. David may have forgotten that for a time, but he remembered.

David called for his pastor, Abiathar the priest, and asked him to help him seek the Lord. One of the reasons you need to be a faithful part of a local church, is that you need somewhere and someone who will be there to help you in a time of need. Hopefully, your pastor is a faithful and godly leader who can speak godly wisdom into your life and help escort you into the presence of God if you have strayed. David called for spiritual counsel and sought the Lord. You don't have to wait until you are in trouble to seek Him; but, when you are, there's no better place you can turn. Notice David's prayer to the Lord. This is the prayer of a seeker. He's not bringing a laundry list of things he wants God to do for him. He's not telling God his plans. He is seeking God's will and God's plan. David prayed, "God, what would you have me do?" That's the attitude of faith God may be looking for in you. No demands -- no vain promises -- just a humble heart seeking His heart.

Then, upon receiving the revealed will of God,

David sprang into action. Armed with only 600 men and a promise, David set out after the enemy. God had promised to be faithful, and David was taking God at His word. God is always faithful to His Word. The Bible assures us that all the promises of God are "Yes" in Christ (2 Cor. 1:20). He has always and will always be faithful to His Word.

The burning of Ziklag represented the consequences of David's sin. He was in the wrong place, trusting in the wrong people, and about to fight in the wrong battle. Ultimately, David had put himself in a position of volunteering to fight against God. God allowed Ziklag to be burned in order to point out to David that he was out of God's will for his life. It might be that God will have to do that in your life. God may have to burn your Ziklag to get you where He wants you to be so that you're ready to do His will. Are you living in enemy territory? Don't be surprised if God doesn't allow circumstances in your life to get your attention to bring you back to Him. No matter how it may seem, God is working for your good. Don't wait until you feel like you have nowhere to turn. Trust Him today. That's how to be a man after God's Heart.

A Man After God's Heart Is Known by His Character

3

"The Lord sought for Himself a man after His own heart and appointed him as leader of His people" (1 Sam. 13:14).

There are four passages in Scripture that highlight God's search for a man and the discovery in David of the kind of man God was seeking.[24] These passages are 1 Samuel 13:14; Psalm 89:20; Acts 7:46; and 13:22. The passages reveal what God was seeking and what He found in David. In each of those four occasions, something significant to becoming a man after God's own heart is revealed. Any man who wishes to attract God's attention should strive to model the attributes that the God's Word indicates caught God's eye.

What first caught God's eye about David was his heart. David is described as a "man after God's heart." No one else in Scripture is given this description. Not Noah, Abraham, Moses, Joseph, Job, or even Daniel in the Old Testament, nor Peter, John, or Paul in the New. This description was reserved for only one man. That's not to say that there weren't other men in Scripture who were righteous, or even faithful. But, it does indicate something significant about David.

The phrase that is used of David is an unusual description in Scripture. The only other Old Testament use of the phrase "according to his heart" is found in Deut. 20:8. However, in that text, it is not God's heart that is being referenced. Rather, in that context, the phrase is used to refer to the influence one person might have on others. The context is regarding a military setting with men being sent into battle. The officer was instructed to weed out anyone who was fearful so that he would not negatively influence others to have a heart "like his heart." Moses' instructions were for the protection of the people. The officer was to safeguard his unit, so that anyone who was fainthearted would not infect the motivation of the others. The use of the phrase "like his heart" reflected the fear that was on the inside. In other words, what was really there.

You and I can cover up what's in our hearts or try to pretend it's not there; but, if it's in your heart, it is who you are. David, in his heart, was like the heart of God. Something about his heart was something like something about the heart of God. The text provides for us the starting point.

A Man After God's Heart Loves and Keeps God's Word

The end of the verse gives us a clue about what God approved: "because you have not kept the Lord's command." Saul was rejected because he was unfaithful to God's Word. On the contrary, David was selected upon the anticipation of his faithfulness. David was known for his love of God's Word. This can be most clearly seen in the longest song of David's that we have. In Psalm 119, David mentioned God's Word 110 times in 176 verses. He uses X different words to describe God's Word. He talked of God's law, testimonies, precepts, statutes, judgments, commandments, Word, and ordinances. In this psalm, David reveals his love for God's Word and his passion to understand it. He knew his need for God's Word that was forever established (89-90). David reiterated his love for God's Word eleven times in this psalm (47, 48, 97, 113, 119, 127, 140, 159, 163, 165, and 167), and also pledged his allegiance to God's Word (5, 8, 10, 11, 15, 17, 22, 31, 32, 33, 34, 51, 55, 56, 57, 59, 60, 61, 67, 69, 87, 88, 100, 101, 102, 105, 106, 110, 112, 129, 141, 145, 146, 157, 166, 168). The king professed to: meditate on God's Word (23, 27, 48, 78, 99, 148), trust in God's Word (42), seek God's Word (45, 94), speak of God's Word (46), hope in God's Word (49), take comfort in God's Word (50, 76), remember God's Word (16, 52, 83, 93, 109, 153, 176), sing of God's Word (54), desire to learn God's Word (64, 68, 71, 73, 108, 124, 125, 135,

144, 169), believe in God's Word (66), delight in God's Word (70, 77, 92, 123, 143, 174), wait for God's Word (74, 81, 114, 147), consider God's Word (95), learn from God's Word (104), rejoice in God's Word (111, 162), fear God's Word (120), esteem God's Word (128), long for God's Word (131), know God's Word (152), stand in awe of God's Word (161), and have chosen God's Word (173). What is the nature of your relationship with God's Word? Do you have a love and a longing for God's Word? A man after God's heart loves and keeps His Word.

Let me hasten to add, you can't have the love God wants you to have for His Word unless you are faithfully spending time reading it, memorizing it, hearing it, learning it, and applying it. God has promised that His Word never returns void. It always accomplishes the purpose for which God intended it.[25] It might be that part of that purpose is the difference God wants to make in your life through His Word.

If you want to be a man after God's heart, you must learn God's Word and you must apply it to your life. Scripture pronounces blessings on all who read, hear, and heed God's Word. If you want His blessing, you must follow His heart; and you find it through His Word.

A Character Formed by Covenant

David's love of God's Word and obedience to it was just part of a character that pleased God. In fact, the text in 1 Samuel 13:14 reveals that even before his reign began, David's character pleased God. He was a man who demonstrated his faith by how he lived. He had a heart like His. In contrast to Saul, David would do according to God's commandments.

First Chronicles 17 is a very significant chapter in the Old Testament, and, in fact, for all of history. It is here that God affirms His covenant with David. Upon hearing of God's great Promise for His life, David prays a prayer of gratitude and humility. In it, David acknowledges that it is according to God's heart that He has done all that He has done (1 Chron. 17:19). David concludes by stating that his prayer is an expression of his own heart in agreement with the heart of God. In essence, David is saying, "My heart is in tune with yours" (1 Chron. 17:25). God agreed. Could you say the same thing about your heart?

David's son, Solomon, would later affirm that the heart of his father was right before God (2 Chron. 6:8). He knew that the reason for God's grace in his life and that of his father was because of the faithfulness of David's heart. David's heart was like God's heart. So, what is God's heart like?

What God's Word Says about God's Heart

The other references in Scripture to God's heart give us a clue as to what is being said about David as a man after

God's heart. First, Scripture records that God was grieved in His heart because of the sin of mankind (Gen. 6:6). So, the heart of God is pure and grieved by sin. Second, at the dedication of the Temple, God declared that His eyes and heart will be in the Temple (1 Kings 9:3). So, the heart of God loves worship. Third, in 1 Chronicles 17:19, when God made a covenant with David which included the promise of the Messiah, David realized that God's covenant was with him because of God's heart. So, God's heart is full of grace. Fourth, the Psalmist declared that the plans of God's heart stand forever (Ps. 33:11). So, God's heart is consistent and dependable. Fifth, the prophet Jeremiah recorded that God's judgment will continue until He has performed the thoughts of His heart (Jer. 30:24). So, God's heart is faithful to His Word. Finally, the weeping prophet declared that even in judgment, God's heart yearns for His wayward people (Jer. 31:20). So, God's heart is compassionate.

God's heart reflects the holiness of His nature, the indwelling of His presence, the faithfulness of His promise, the consistency of His character, the certainly of His Word, and the compassion of His soul. So, if David's heart is like God's heart, what does that reveal about David's heart?

Scripture reveals that the heart of God represents the center of His emotion, His character, and His intention. Thus, for David to be described as a man after God's heart suggests the affection God had for David and the obedience David showed to God. Even more, it implies

that David's character was like that of God. We see
this most clearly in David's repentance. We've already
conceded that David was not a perfect man. However,
there's no better example of repentance in Scripture than
what we find exemplified in David.

When David was confronted regarding his sin with
Bathsheba and Uriah, David poured out his heart before
the Lord. David's words to Nathan in 2 Samuel 12:13,
"I have sinned against the Lord," only begin to express
his contrition before the Lord. Later, in Psalm 51, David
poured out his heart before the Lord in humility and
repentance. Consider his requests of the Lord:

"Have mercy on me, O God"
"Wash away all my iniquity"
"For I know my transgressions"
"Against you, you only have I sinned"
"Purge me with hyssop"
"Make me hear joy and gladness"
"Hide Your face from my sins"
"Create in me a clean heart"
"Do not cast me from Your presence"
"Restore to me the joy of Your salvation"
"Deliver me from the guilt of bloodshed"
These are the cries of a repentant man.

David displayed a similar spirit when he was confronted with his sin in taking a census. At this point,
David had been king for thirty-eight years, and, once

> *A heart like God's heart cannot live unconvicted with unrepentant sin.*

again, grew complacent in his walk with the Lord. The problem wasn't so much what he did; after all, the Lord had instructed him to take a census previously. The problem was that he acted without consulting the Lord -- much like when, in his eagerness to move the Ark the first time, he tried to do things for God without consulting God. In his sin, God took measures to get David's attention.

The Bible says that even before the Prophet, Gad confronted him that his heart condemned him (2 Sam. 24:10). A heart like God's heart cannot live unconvicted with unrepentant sin. David's heart, the heart that was like God's heart, was conscience-stricken and broken before the Lord. David cried out to the Lord, "I have sinned greatly in what I have done; but now, I pray, O LORD, take away the iniquity of Your servant, for I have done very foolishly" (10). Even before God's messenger came, David's heart was broken because of his sin. He would later cry out to the Lord under the weight of the consequences of his sin, "Surely I have sinned, and I have done wickedly; but these sheep, what have they done? Let Your hand, I pray, be against me and against my father's house" (17). The opposite is seen in Saul.

I Did It MY Way

The contrast in the Bible between Saul and David is striking. Consider the differences between Israel's first and second kings:

- David kept the word of the Lord (1 Chron. 14:16); Saul did not (1 Chron. 10:13)
- David was willing to wait on God's timing for his life, waiting at least ten years to become king after he was informed of it by Samuel and another seven and a half years to become king over all of Israel (2 Sam.5:1-5); Saul was impatient and unwilling to wait on God (1 Sam. 13)
- Saul was jealous of David's success (1 Sam. 18:9); David was willing to serve Saul as king even after being told that he was going to be king (1 Samuel 16)
- David was courageous (1 Samuel 17); Saul was cowardly (1 Sam. 17; 18:12, 15; cf. 27:4),
- David was concerned about genuine worship of the Lord through the Ark of the Covenant (2 Samuel 6); Saul wasn't and never incorporate the Ark during his reign[26]
- When confronted by the prophet in his sin, David repented (2 Samuel 12); Saul made excuses and tried to cover it up (1 Sam. 13:8-14; 15:1-30)
- David trusted God in battle (1 Sam. 17; 23:9-14; Saul trusted in his weapons and armor

(1 Samuel 17)

- David inquired of the Lord prior to going into battle (1 Chron. 14:10); Saul consulted a medium (1 Samuel 28)[27]

- David, twice, showed mercy to Saul (1 Samuel 24; 26); Saul didn't show mercy to David (1 Sam. 18:9, 21; 19:1, 9-10, 11-17, 18-23; 20:30; 23:10-12, 15, 19-28; 24:1-22; 25:44; 26:1-25; 27:4)

- David refused to kill Saul with a spear when he had the chance and even felt remorse for cutting off the edge of Saul's robe (1 Sam. 24:5); Saul tried to kill David with a spear and felt no remorse (1 Sam. 18:11; 19:10)

- David referred to Him as "My God" (2 Sam. 22:7); Saul referred to the Lord as "your God" (1 Sam. 15:15)

- When David didn't exactly get what he wanted from the Lord, he trusted that the Lord's way was better (2 Samuel 7); when Saul didn't get what he wanted from the Lord, he got angry (1 Sam. 18:10-11)

- David was willing to trust the Lord regarding his elevation to the throne (1 Sam. 26:9-10); Saul tried to manipulate circumstances to remain king (1 Sam. 20:31)

- When the Spirit of the Lord left Saul, He inhabited David (1 Sam. 16:13-14)

- God blessed David (1 Chron. 14); God killed

Saul (1 Chron. 10:14)

• David defeated the Philistines in battle (1 Samuel 17); Saul died fighting against them (1 Samuel 31)

One could argue that the sins David committed were as egregious if not more than those committed by Saul. Perhaps, that is the case; although, the Scripture does not focus as closely on the life of Saul as it does that of David. Yet, even that is not the issue. David is not considered a man after God's heart because he was better than everybody else. The key was that David's heart was like that of God. Even when David sinned against God, he turned back to Him in repentance and faith. Saul was much the opposite.

One of the tendencies of Saul in Scripture was that he tended to try to do his own will and pass it off as God's. A closer examination of the life of Saul demonstrates a consistent pattern of not seeking God. The first time Saul appeared in Scripture, he was with his servant searching for his father's donkeys. But, when they could not find the donkeys, it was the servant who instructed Saul to seek the Lord through the Prophet. That typifies a pattern in Saul of refusing to seek the Lord which later became the cause of his rejection as King and, ultimately, his death.

Early into his reign, Saul was rejected by God (the first time) for insincere worship. On the verge of a battle with the Philistines, Saul wanted Samuel to bless Israel.

However, Samuel was delayed, and Saul grew impatient. The King offered a sacrifice to invoke God's blessing on his military. Scripture records that immediately upon completing the sacrifice, Samuel arrived. Even when confronted by the Prophet, Saul tells a half-truth to Samuel and seems unfazed by the Prophet's rebuke. On this occasion, the Lord declared that Saul's dynasty was removed. Jonathan, Saul's son, would ultimately pay the consequences for his father's sin.

In that same event, Saul demonstrated a fundamental failure as a leader. He seems to have thought only about himself. As the King, it was his responsibility for the people to be ready for battle; however, the Bible records that when the inventory of weapons was taken, only Saul and Jonathan had swords with them. The Philistines had a monopoly on blacksmiths. A wise leader would have prepared his troops for battle.

Sandwiched between the two stories of Saul's rejection by God are two pericopies that typify his reign. The first came on the occasion of a foolish vow by Saul in the midst of a battle with the Philistines. Saul vowed that anyone who ate anything before the battle was completed would be executed. Saul's son, Jonathan was not there when his father made the vow. Jonathan, along with his armor-bearer, was out winning a significant battle for his father. While on the battle field exhausted and hungry Jonathan dipped the end of his staff into a honeycomb and ate some honey. When Jonathan was told about Saul's vow, he responded, "My father has troubled the land. Look now, how my countenance has brightened because I tasted a little of this honey" (1 Sam 14:29). Later, when Jonathan's act was discovered, Saul compounded his rash oath by intending to kill his innocent son.

Despite Jonathan's disagreement with his father's vow, he was willing to submit to the vow made by his father, the King. It was only the intercession of the people that prevented Saul from carrying out Jonathan's death. One wonders, if Saul felt so strongly about a vow to the Lord, why he was so easily talked out of it. The passage highlights Saul's foolish attempts at vain piety and weak leadership.

The other passage set between the two accounts of God's rejection of King Saul indicates the arrogance of King Saul. Despite having just been rebuked by the Prophet, Samuel in 1 Samuel 15, and informed that he and his family would suffer the consequences of his sin, Saul was busy erecting a monument to himself![28] Contrast the arrogance of King Saul, who wanted to build a monument to himself, and the humility of King David, who desired to build a Temple to the Lord.

The occasion of Saul's final rejection from the Lord as King marked another attempt by Saul to disobey God while trying to appear religious. The Israelites were in battle with the Amalekites. Israel defeated them, and God's instructions were to completely destroy them. However, Saul had another idea. When Samuel came on the scene, his first indication that Saul had violated God's instructions was the sound of sheep that had not been killed. Next, the Prophet learned that Saul had spared the King of the Amalekites. Saul, again, pretended to have a religious reason for his disobedience, as though his plan was better than that of God. He told Samuel that he had spared the sheep to make a sacrifice to God. Maybe, like Saul, you've held back on God and kept some of the best parts of your life for yourself. You can try to make it sound religious, but God knows your heart.

Samuel reminded the disobedient King, that God would rather have his obedience than his sacrifice. Samuel killed the Amalekite King, and God rejected the Israelite King (1 Sam. 15:1-34).

The result of God's absence brought severe consequences for King Saul. Not only would his son lose the opportunity to reign as King, the loss of God's presence resulted in the frequent presence of evil spirits tormenting Saul. Saul knew he was being oppressed; however, instead of using that as an occasion to return to God in repentance, Saul simply tried to resolve the situation on his own. He hired David, an accomplished musician, to come and play music for him. When David, who was possessed by the Spirit of God, played music for the King, who was rejected by God, the evil spirits left Saul. Indeed, how tragic it is when we fail to note God's judgment and miss an opportunity to return to Him (1 Sam. 16:13-23).

The occasion of David's most notable victory was also a very telling experience for King Saul. God used David as His agent to bring victory to Israel. However, the ironic truth of the story is that Saul should have been the one to engage the giant in battle. He was the King; he was the military leader; he was head and shoulders taller than all the people of Israel. For nearly seven weeks the people of Israel looked to their leader for direction, and he cowardly failed them.

Ironically, even when Saul "allowed" David to fight his battles for him, Saul still wanted David to fight Saul's giant Saul's way. To be fair, Saul thought he was being helpful. He dressed David up in his own armor – probably, the finest armor Israel had. But, David knew something that Saul didn't. This giant wouldn't be defeated by mankind's strength but by the Lord's.

What would have happened had Saul trusted in God to win the battle like David did? I believe God would have used him to bring the victory. What would happen if you and I trusted God in our battles like David did in his? Saul's cowardice and lack of faith cost him the reputation of the people, the delay of a national victory, the glamour of being the subject of folksongs (for which he would later be jealous), and the reputation of being a giant-killer (1 Sam. 17:1-58).

Looking for God in All the Wrong Places

The Goliath-event had a lingering effect for both David and Saul. David became a folk hero. The Bible records that, the women came out from all the cities of Israel to meet King Saul, singing and dancing with tambourines, with shouts of joy, and with three-stringed instruments. As they celebrated, the women sang, "Saul has killed his thousands, but David has killed his tens of thousands" (1 Sam. 18:6-7). Uh oh. The people came "from all the cities of Israel to meet Saul" but sang songs recognizing David as the real hero. Saul understood that the women had given David the honor over him and became very jealous. Note the series of events that immediately unfolded when Saul allowed himself to grow jealous of another's success: "So Saul watched David jealously from that day forward. The next day an evil spirit from God took control of Saul, and he began to rave inside the palace" (1 Sam. 18:9-10). This would be the occasion of Saul's first attempt to kill David. A jealous spirit will lead to sin. Instead of rejoicing with David and praising for his success, Saul's jealousy controlled him for most of the rest of his life.

What do you do what you need to hear from God? The Bible gives us the clear instructions: "Call to Me and I will answer you and show you great and mighty things that you do not know" (Jer. 33:3). Saul needed to hear from the Lord. But, he had made a pattern of doing things his own way and trying to make them appear spiritual. So, when he desperately needed to hear from God and Samuel was no longer alive, Saul took matters into his own hands -- again! Instead of seeking God in prayer, he sought a medium in a desperate attempt to conjure up Samuel to get the dead Prophet to give him a word from the Lord. He received a word all right, but it wasn't the one that he wanted.

Saul was looking for God in all the wrong places. Now, he had gone too far. He opted to use unspiritual means to try to receive spiritual truth. Upon Samuel's appearance, Saul indicated to him that God was silent. God wasn't speaking to the king "neither by prophets nor by dreams" (1 Sam. 28:15). The Bible doesn't record any attempt by the Saul to consult the prophets in an effort to hear from the Lord. However, it would fit in his character to expect God to come find him. When God didn't speak, the King called on the last man to relay to him the Lord's message, even though he was dead. It was as though Saul was saying to Samuel, "I know you are dead, but this is more important. Stop what you are doing and come talk to me again because God won't." Even though the Prophet was dead, Saul still expected Samuel to serve Saul. Saul called on a medium, although he had previously made their existence illegal in the kingdom, and insisted that she contact Samuel to deliver a message from God to Saul. Shockingly, God obliged and gave him another opportunity to hear His message. Only this time, the message from God to the King was one of judgment.

Mene, Mene, Tekel, Upharsin

Like King Belshazzar in Daniel's day, Saul had been
weighed in the balance and found wanting. Samuel informed King Saul that his days were numbered. In fact,
"day" should be singular. The prophet declared that
within a day, Saul would be with him in death (1 Sam.
28:19). Not exactly the same encouragement that Jesus
gave to the repentant thief on the cross, "Today you will
be with me in paradise" (Luke 23:43).

When one examines the passages in Scripture that
focus on Saul, it becomes apparent that from the very
beginning, he was a man who was unprepared to lead,
short-sighted, unwilling to listen, and made poor decisions. The first time that we encountered Saul in
Scripture, he demonstrated a lack of preparation for his
journey and had to borrow money from his own servant
to complete their journey (1 Sam. 9:1-10).

After that initial encounter with Samuel, Saul was
made King over Israel. Early in his reign, Saul encountered a challenge in the form of the Philistines. It was
customary for the King to secure the blessing of the
Prophet and to offer sacrifices to the Lord prior to going to battle. However, on this occasion, Samuel was
delayed. The people were becoming increasingly fearful of the Philistines, threatening to run away, and Saul
was growing impatient. So, Saul offered the sacrifices
himself, instead of waiting for the Prophet. Immediately
upon his completion of the sacrifice, Samuel arrived.

Saul seemed oblivious to the gravity of his disobedience. It was then that Samuel explained to the King,

> You have acted foolishly; you have not kept the commandment of the Lord your God, which He commanded you, for now the Lord would have established your kingdom over Israel forever. But now your kingdom shall not endure. The Lord has sought out for Himself a man after His own heart, and the Lord has appointed him as ruler over His people because you have not kept what the Lord commanded you (1 Sam. 13:13-14).

Immediately following Saul's disobedience in the sacrifice, we find another occasion in which Saul fails his soldiers, and indeed, Israel, by demonstrating a lack of preparation for battle. Israel was bereft of blacksmiths, so anyone needing a tool sharpened or a weapon made had to travel to the land of the Philistines and pay their enemies for those services. The result was that "on the day of battle that neither sword nor spear was found in the hands of any of the people who were with Saul and Jonathan" (1 Sam. 13:16-23). That fundamental failure to take care of the details typified Saul's ineptitude as a leader.

Saul's next failure, as already shown, nearly cost his son, Jonathan his life. Now, there are several problems with Saul's reaction to Jonathan's innocent action. Most notably, was Saul's determination to put his son to death for a curse of which he was not aware (1 Sam. 14:24-46).

Nevertheless, even if Saul felt that strongly about putting Jonathan to death for his own foolish vow, how is it he is so easily talked out of it by the people? One wonders if Saul was not about to execute his son simply to save face in front of the people by not breaking his vow.

The next chapter outlines Saul's ultimate rejection as king over Israel. When Saul offered a sacrifice instead of waiting on Samuel, the Lord declared that his kingdom had been removed. It was here when Samuel reminded the King, "To obey is better than sacrifice" (1 Sam. 15:22). Saul lost his Kingdom and the lesson was reinforced that God takes sin very seriously.

The next indication of Saul's inability to lead God's people came in his failure to note God's absence in his life. The Bible strikingly states that "the spirit of the Lord departed from Saul" (1 Sam. 16:14). Concurrent with the Holy Spirit's absence in Saul's life emerged the presence of an evil spirit which tormented him. Jesus told a very similar story about a man who cleansed his life of an evil spirit, but failed to fill his life with God's Spirit. Instead of leaving the man alone, the spirit that was expelled went out and found seven spirit, more evil than itself, which all came and inhabited the man. Jesus concluded that in the end, his last state was much worse than his first (Matt. 12:45). The lesson is clear; we must be filled with God's Holy Spirit, or we are vulnerable to the evil spirits of this world.

Tragically, when God's Spirit departed from Saul, he didn't recognize it. He seemed only to discover the

Spirit's absence when his servants pointed it out to them. How bad must Saul's condition have been for his servants to notice that he was oppressed by evil spirits? And, yet, instead of repenting and turning back to the Lord, Saul and his servants concocted a plan to relieve his distress. They would hire someone to play soothing music in Saul's presence to exorcise the evil spirits. Enter David with his harp. Clearly, the presence of God's Spirit in David overcame the evil of the spirits distressing the King. Perhaps, this was the Lord giving Saul an opportunity to recognize the Lord's absence and repent. Instead, Saul preferred to strategize a way around God's absence. He wanted God's presence his own way. But, you and I can't have God's way if we are unwilling to give up our own.

Saul's inadequacy as a leader was further exemplified in the experience with Goliath. While the story is about David's success against the giant, it also reveals Saul's failure. While David trusted in God, Saul only trusted in his army. While David showed courage, Saul showed cowardice. While David demonstrated anger at the Lord's armies being taunted, Saul demonstrated desperation in his willingness to let anybody fight the giant but him. David's testimony that "The Lord ... will deliver me" (1 Sam. 17:37) should have shamed the once faithful King, but didn't seem to faze him.

Once David brought the success to Israel that should have been won by Saul, the people began to see what was lacking in their King. Women began to sing songs about David's prowess as a leader who overshadowed Saul. Here, Saul demonstrated another significant character flaw. While he wasn't willing to risk fighting the giant, he still wanted the glory for the victory. Instead, when the accolades began to fall to David, Saul became jealous. This young man, who had previously soothed the evil spirits and killed the evil giants, now became despised by the now evil King of Israel. It was after this that Saul began to strategize ways to eliminate David. It turned him against his daughter, Michal; his son, Jonathan; his servant, David; his priest, Ahimelech; the nation of Israel; and ultimately, God. Even after David twice spared Saul's life, Saul continued to attempt to take David's. Saul lived the rest of his life in David's shadow and died chasing David and pursuing the glory against the Philistines that he felt he lost in the valley of Elah when he "cowered" in the presence of a giant and "soured" in the victory of someone else.

A final example of Saul's departure from the Lord and abdication of his leadership as King is seen in his desperation to once again find God on his own terms. After Samuel died, there was no one who would tell the King the truth about God's expectations. It was here that Saul turned to the medium in a tragic attempt to hear from the Lord. How arrogant and desperate! Even when he wanted to hear from God, he wanted it on his own terms. This was the last straw. Samuel did, in fact, bring Saul a message from the Lord. But, it was not the message Saul wanted to hear. Instead it was a message of his impending doom. Samuel declared that within a day, Saul would be killed. What a tragic end to a promising and once-faithful king.

Do You See What I See?

"...Our hearts must be synthesized with His."

God is not concerned about what you can do for Him. He is concerned about what He can do in and through you. Both David and Saul were imperfect men. What made David a man after God's heart? The answer is found in Samuel's message of judgment to Saul. He told the king, "You have not kept the commandment of the Lord your God, which He commanded you" (1 Sam. 13:13). The bottom line is, Saul refused to do what God commanded. He refused to do it God's way.

Consequently, God was looking for a man after His heart; a man who would do what God desired. In 1 Samuel 13:14, we find Samuel's rebuke of Saul. In God's rejection of Saul, we learn some keys to God's selection of David. In it are keys to how we can have a character that pleases God. The first lesson you and I need to learn from David about capturing God's attention is that our hearts must be synthesized with His. That means that there should be harmony between our hearts and His. The Bible is describing the character of the man God is seeking. The Bible tells us in 1 Kings 11:4 that the heart of David was loyal to God. Samuel told Saul that God was looking for a man who had a heart like that of God. That doesn't mean that David was perfect. It just means that his heart was like God's. My friend, it is still true that "The Lord does not look at the things man looks at. Man looks at the outward appearance, but the Lord looks at the heart."

The Bible says in Gen. 1:26 that mankind is made in the image of God. That means that something about man is something like something about God. It doesn't mean that God is like me. It means that I am something like God.

A similar analogy existed with David's heart. Scripture isn't saying that God's heart was like David's heart. We know David wasn't perfect. We've seen that David sinned against the Lord. Yet, something about

"...Our purposes must be sacrificed to His."

David's heart was something like something about God's heart. Many scholars have tried to speculate about what it was about David's heart that was like that of God's. I believe the answer is found in the second thing Samuel pointed out that God was looking for in a leader.

Do you see what kind of man God was seeking? It's important to note that the Lord hasn't changed His standards. He is still looking for a man after His heart to accomplish His purpose. Before He wanted what David could do, He wanted who David could be.

The second lesson you and I need to learn from this passage is that our purposes must be sacrificed to His. You can't follow God and go your own way. If you are going to be a man after God's heart, you have to follow His heart. Whatever plans David may have had for his life were submitted to those that God had for him. David was appointed for the task that God had for him. It works the same for you. Not only are you the man for whom God is looking, but God has given you the ability to accomplish His purpose. He has already equipped you with everything you need to carry out His will. The key is you have to do it His way. Indeed, you are only effective when you are serving how and where God has appointed you.

Three of our boys have surrendered their lives to full-time Christian service. One of them, who made that decision during church camp explained to us that the Lord used one of the songs that they sang during the week to soften his heart. The lyrics of the song were:

Ruin my life the plans I have made
Ruin desires for my own selfish gain
Destroy the idols that have taken Your place
'Till it's You alone I live for,
You alone I live for.[29]

Are you willing for the Lord to change your plans? What if God's will for you isn't the same as your will for you? In John 9, the disciples came to Jesus to ask why a certain man was born blind. They wanted to know if it was on account of his sin or the sins of his parents. Jesus responded, "neither ... but that the works of God may be revealed in Him" (9:10). You are who you are for a purpose; God's purpose.

Look again at what the text says about David. He was appointed by God. We've already seen that the Lord was the initiating force in the story. The Lord sought out a man for Himself and the Lord appointed him. In the same way, the Lord has already chosen the path that He wants for you. Paul told the church in Philippi, "It is the Lord who is at work in you both to will and to do for His good pleasure" (Phil. 2:13). It's not about what you want or your purpose. It's about what God wants. He has chosen you. He has commanded you. How will you respond? God is looking for a man in you who will accomplish His purpose.

God was also seeking in a king someone who would do as He commanded. Along with someone after God's heart, God was also looking for a leader who was willing to be led. Note the repetition of the word, "commanded" in verses 13 and 14. Saul was told that he had not kept the commandments which he was commanded. Conversely, the Prophet declared that God had commanded a man to be a commander who would do what He commanded. God was commanding a man who would be a commander and do what He commanded.

A third lesson we all need to learn from this text

is that our desires must be surrendered to His. Samuel told Saul that God was looking for a man who would be committed to His commands. Saul was looking for loopholes. He wanted some excuse to do what he wanted instead of what God wanted. Think about it, he sacrificed his kingdom because he was impatient. He wasn't even willing to wait a few minutes on God's time. As soon as things didn't turn out the way that Saul wanted or how he planned, he was ready to skip God's plan and start doing His own. What about you? When God's plans don't turn out exactly as you anticipated are you still committed to follow them?

God was looking for a man who would lead as he was instructed; who would command as he had been commanded. The word that Samuel used could be translated to mean that Saul had not guarded what the Lord had instructed him to do. It meant that God was looking for someone who would seek God's will, but also keep God's will. God was looking for someone who would follow Him. Most of us men like the commanding part, but not so much the part about being under command.

The reason Saul was rejected by God as king was because he wanted his way more than God's way. What about you? Are you pursuing God's path and plan for your life? God has a will and a plan that is already laid out for you. God is looking for a man in you who will follow His commands. That's the character of the man for whom God is seeking.

You Are the Man God is Looking For

If you are a man who is pursuing God's Heart, there are a few lessons from God's selection of David that are important for you to remember. First, you are the man for whom God is looking. Too often, we get the idea that God can't use me because of _____. Maybe you fill in that blank with an action, an attitude, a habit, a failure. It doesn't matter what you include in that blank, it's still just an excuse. It's not that God *might* want to use you, or even that He *could* use you. The answer is that God *would* use you and *will* use you if you submit to Him.

The answer is not in you getting better for God. The answer if found in your submission to Him. You are just the man for whom God is looking. King Saul is a lesson on wasted potential. Remember when he first became King. Imagine all of the possibilities. He looked good. He had the right attitude. He got the best advice. He started well. He was even chosen by God. God told Samuel, "He is the man of whom I spoke to you" (1 Sam. 9:17). Indeed, the Bible even declared that the Spirit of the Lord was upon him (1 Sam. 10:6). So, what happened? Somewhere along the way, Saul stopped looking for what God wanted and began pursing what he wanted. God is looking for a man in you who will pursue His heart.

Becoming the Man God is Seeking

There was an experience early in David's reign as King that reinforces the importance of doing it God's way versus doing it our own way. In 2 Samuel 6, David has just recently received a promotion. For 10 years after his anointing as Saul's successor, he was on the run for his life. Finally, he was made king over what was only a small part of Saul's former kingdom. He was king over the tribe of Judah. Upon his anointing over Judah, David made an appeal to the other tribes of Israel to recognize his coronation. However, Saul's former chief military commander, Abner, made Saul's son, Ish-Bosheth king instead (2:1-11).

Later, in 2 Samuel 5, David is finally made king over all Israel. The parallel account in 1 Chronicles 10 indicates that it was at the initiative of the rest of Israel to request that David become the king over a united Israel. David relocated his capital from Hebron to Jerusalem to geographically position his capital at the center of the nation, on a secure mountain, and a key crossroads of the kingdom.

One of David's first acts as king over all Israel was to seek to bring the Ark of the Covenant back into Israel's worship. During the reign of King Saul, the Ark was conspicuously absent. David knew that the Ark represented God's presence.[30] Previously, the Ark accompanied the children of Israel in the wilderness (Num. 10:33), was carried into the Jordan river a Sabbath day's journey ahead of the people as they crossed on dry ground (Josh. 3:6-17; 4:7-10), went before them into battle (Josh. 6:6-8), served as a visible representation of God's covenant with His people (Josh. 8:30-35), represented the place where Israel could inquire of God (Judg. 20:27), was used as representation to Israel's enemies that God's presence was with them (1 Sam. 4:3), and was a place of sacrifice on the Mercy Seat which sat on the cover of the ark (Exod. 25:17-22).

Inside the Ark of the Covenant were three very precious reminders of how Israel was set apart unto the Lord: the Ten Commandments, the rod of Aaron, and a jar of manna (Heb. 9:4). Those three ingredients represented God's covenant, His protection, and His provision. When the Tabernacle was erected and later, when the Temple was completed, the Ark of the Covenant was kept in the Holy of Holies. The Ark wasn't just special it was holy.

As David prepared to relocate the Ark, he made what sounds like a good decision, but went about it the wrong way. David sought advice before moving the Ark. Seeking sound advice is always a good idea. Unfortunately, those whom David sought were not the ones able to give him the advice he needed. Always that warrior, instead of seeking advice from his religious leaders, David sought counsel from his military. Not surprisingly, his military was eager to fulfill the instructions of their king. In fact, the proposal seemed "right in the eyes of the people" (1 Chron. 13:4). Consulting the military on military matters is prudent; however, for spiritual matters one would think that seeking David's spiritual counselors would have been a better recourse. It was a bad strategy on how to accomplish a good idea.

Armed with the support of his people, the king took measures to transport the Ark. When David wanted to bring the Ark to Jerusalem he sent an army of 30,000 chosen men to retrieve it. These were not just regular soldiers; they were David's Special Forces.

For 50 years, the Ark of the Covenant had been at the home of Abinadab. The Ark was taken there before Saul became king. For the entire 40 years of Saul's reign, the Ark of God was forgotten. During that time, Samuel records that all of Israel "lamented after the Lord" (1 Sam. 7:2) because of the absence of the Lord among them. Early in David's period in office, he sent to bring the Ark to Jerusalem. So, the king's 30,000 soldiers made the ten mile journey to bring it to the palace.

Abinadab's two sons, Uzzah and Ahio, accompany the Ark. Their family has been the caretakers of the Ark for more than a generation. No doubt their family has been blessed by the physical presence of the Ark among them. David accompanies the army as they begin to transport the Ark. The excitement was growing, David was dancing, instruments were playing, the people were celebrating, and Abinadab's two boys were leading the parade.

The excitement soon turned to tragedy when the procession encountered a bump along the way. To transport the Ark, David had chosen a new cart. The oxen pulled the cart and Uzzah and Ahio walked on either side. All went well until the bump. Maybe the oxen didn't see it, or maybe the two boys were too busy celebrating and missed it, but when the cart hit the bump, the Ark became unsteady. It's understandable what Uzzah did; many of us would have the same instinctive reaction. When something is about to fall, the natural thing is to try to steady it. That's what Uzzah did. He stretched out his hand to steady the Ark, and when he touched it, God struck him dead.

Bible students sometimes struggle with God's outburst against Uzzah. David did, too. In fact, David changed the name of the place where God struck Uzzah to Perez-Uzzah, "the breakthough [of God] against Uzzah." The Bible even records that David was afraid of the Lord (9). But wait. Look more carefully at the story.

Surely David knew the law. The law included very specific instructions for moving the Ark (Exod. 25:12-15). In fact, the law clearly stipulates that if someone touched the Ark, they would die (Num. 4:15). Maybe the king forgot. Maybe with all the chaos of a recent promotion, David just didn't give it enough careful thought. Maybe he thought providing a new cart would be better. At least it was new! Whatever his reason, David disguised his disobedience with a shiny substitute. He's spoiled by a new cart. No matter how much better you think your plans are than God's, it's likely He won't agree.

Uzzah should have known that. They had been the caretakers of the Ark for half a century. How is it that he has become so comfortable around the holy that he treats it like any other object? He's too comfortable around the sacred.

David would eventually get it right. A few months after trying to get God's blessings his way, the king tried it God's way. The scene is similar. There's music again. David is again dancing. The people are celebrating. But this time, the Levites were carrying the Ark as the Scripture instructed (1 Chron. 15:26).

The Psalmist, in Psalm 132, recorded the struggle and eventual celebration of restoring the Ark to its rightful place. He vowed not to sleep until "I find a place for the Lord" (5). Later, the Psalmist declared, "we heard of it in Ephrathah, we found it in the field of Jaar" (6). Then he could proclaim, "Arise, O Lord, to your resting place, You and the Ark of Your strength" (10). He would later plead for God's blessing and protection "for Your Servant David's sake" (10), and claim God's promise of a horn of David to come in the form of the Messiah (17). You and I can't presume upon God's promise, when we are living outside of His will.

Not everybody got it. They usually don't. The Bible records that David's wife, Michal, was watching the celebration from her window. The saw the king dancing wearing only a linen cloth. She thought it was humiliating for him. Or maybe it embarrassed her. She grew up in the palace of Saul and probably thought she knew appropriate kingly decorum. This wasn't it. Kings don't dance semi-nude before all the servant girls. The Chronicler recorded that when she saw David leaping and carrying on, she despised him in her heart (1 Chron. 15:29). But David didn't care. This time his worship of God was genuine.

It might work that way for you. You may find that when you get excited about your worship of the Lord that not everybody shares in the celebration. Some might even resent it. Not everybody will get it. Don't expect everybody to dance, when you follow God's will. But don't stop dancing. Just remember to let Him lead.

What David thought was worship the first time was only disobedience in disguise. It's not true worship if you're not doing it God's way. No matter how good your intentions may be. If you want God to be pleased, then you have to follow God's plan. If not, all the music, and dancing, and carrying on is just for show. The problem wasn't the celebration. It wasn't even David's motive. The problem was that David refused to follow God's way. If you want to be a man after God's heart, you've got to follow His Word.

A Man After God's Heart Leads Through Service

4

I find the story of Abraham's servant intriguing. Genesis 24 records the details of Abraham's search for a bride for his son, Isaac. The Bible records that Abraham is getting older, and, as any father does, wants the best for his son. Perhaps, he is unable to make the journey but entrusts the task to his servant. Verse 2 tells us a couple of things about the servant whom Abraham chose for this task. First, he was the oldest servant in Abraham's house. Second, he was a ruler over all that Abraham had. So, this was a mature and trustworthy servant. This wasn't his first task. He had already proven himself faithful. Now, he was being entrusted with securing Abraham's legacy.

Here's a servant whose entire life has been given in service to another. As far as he knows, the journey for which he has been chosen will bring very little in the way of success for himself. Instead, he is going in the place of another. His job is to find a wife for Isaac. This seems strange in our culture. Even stranger that neither Abraham nor Isaac have any part in the selection. But, consider the level of trust that Abraham has for his servant.

Abraham provides the servant with very specific instructions and makes him swear an oath that he will follow them carefully and completely. After a quick clarification of the possible alternatives, he is off to find a wife for the son of his master. Even more, he is helping to carry out the mandate that God gave to Abraham.

Not much by way of specific instructions are given to the servant: just to go to a general place and find the right woman. The servant develops a strategy on his own (vs. 10) and entreats the blessing of the Lord on the strategy that he has concocted (11-14). The Bible records that before the servant even finished praying, his plan began to unfold exactly as he prayed it would. It didn't either hurt that the woman was beautiful. But, his faithfulness didn't stop there. After the servant reveals himself and the purpose of his journey to Rebekah, the pretty girl at the well, Rebekah runs off to let her parents know what has happened. As soon as the servant realizes that God has blessed his plan, he bows in worship to the Lord (26). Upon being invited to their home, the servant quickly follows.

Food is offered to the servant, who refused to eat before he explains the purpose for his journey. Then, he outlines the instructions that he received from his master, the plan for which he prayed God's blessings, and gives the Lord the appropriate glory for seeing it carried out. When Rebekah's family hears how God has blessed this servant's journey, they can't help but see that this is the hand and will of God. Rebekah's family agrees that she should accompany the servant to become the wife of Isaac but attempted to detain them "a few days, at least ten" before they left (55). Again, refusing to be distracted from his assigned task, the servant persists: "Do not hinder me since the Lord has prospered my way; send me away so that I may go to my master" (56). He had no interest in small talk. He had a job to complete.

So, Rebekah accompanies the servant to Abraham's house; Isaac gets a pretty wife; Abraham begins to see God's plan for his heritage fulfilled; and the servant is never heard from again. One last thing, the servant is never named in the story. He came up with the strategy, he carried it out, he saw God's blessings on his plans, he accomplished the will of his master, and he didn't even get a footnote in the story with his name on it. I imagine that when he returned, he went back to doing what he was doing before. He probably spent the rest of his life serving Abraham since that's what faithful servants do. He was an unknown servant of great influence.

Jesus said in Luke 17:7-9,

Which of you, having a servant plowing or tending sheep, will say to him when he has come in from the field, 'Come at once and sit down to eat'? But will he not rather say to him, 'Prepare something for my supper, and gird yourself and serve me till I have eaten and drunk, and afterward you will eat and drink'? Doeshe thank that servant because he did the things that were commanded him? I think not.

The servants' responsibility is to serve the master. In fact, Jesus went on to say that we are even unprofitable servants if we only do what we were expected to do (17:10). That means we don't deserve special thanks or rewards for doing what is expected of a servant.

"I Have Found My Servant David"

God says of David, "I have found My servant David" (Ps. 89:20). The emphasis is on God's designation of David as God's servant. Twenty-two times in the Old Testament, God uses this phrase to refer to David.[31] Throughout Scripture, God referred to Abraham, Moses, Caleb, David, Job, Eliakim, Isaiah, Israel, Nebuchadnezzar, and Jesus as His servants, but no one earned that title as frequently as David. In addition, David referred to himself as "your servant" eight times when speaking to God; Solomon referred to his father as the Lord's servant nine times; and David is described as God's servant another eight times by others. Surely, if the Bible says something forty-seven times there's a message being communicated!

David was also a servant of great influence. This is just one part of God's fulfillment of His covenant with His people. The Psalmist was extolling God's mercy toward His people. He records the Lord declaring that He had given help to the mighty; He had exalted His chosen One; He had found His servant; and He had anointed him. Moreover, the Lord declared that His hand would establish David; His arm would strengthen him; His faithfulness and mercy would be with him; through His name, David's horn would be exalted. The picture is of the ultimate fulfillment of God's covenant with his people of a coming Messiah through the line of David. God found in David a servant who would impact the world.

The One God Found

People even sang songs about David. The Bible records that the women sang, "Saul has slain his thousands, but David has slain his ten thousands." That song was sung or referenced several times in Scripture (1 Sam. 18:7-8; 21:11; 29:5). Do you remember the context in which that song was first sung? It was right after David's most recognizable accomplishment – the killing of Goliath (Cf. 1 Samuel 17). God brought David to the battle field, but not before the people of Israel had cowered in fear before their enemy for forty days! David didn't come for a fight, but neither did he back away from it.

In the text, the contrast is significant, almost comical. The reader is immediately struck by the differences in the physical descriptions between the two men. Goliath was over nine feet tall! Although David is never described as being short, he is described as being shorter than Saul and significantly shorter than Goliath. Goliath is described as a warrior. David is described as ruddy (or red; probably red-headed) with beautiful eyes. So, one could derive from the text that David was a short, cute, red-head. No wonder Goliath despised him (1 Sam. 17:42). This was a battle between a big, ugly, warrior and a short, cute, red-head![32]

Also significant in the story is the experience attributed to each combatant. David is described as a youth, but Goliath is a warrior and has been a warrior since he was a youth (1 Sam. 17:33). Saul indicated to David that Goliath had been a hero since he was David's age (maybe even before David was born). David's only combat experience came while shepherding his father's sheep. To be sure, killing a lion or a bear is significant, even remarkable, but still not quite the same. The lion and bear didn't have weapons, armor, or even opposable thumbs! It is likely that David had never before been in a battle. Though he had killed animals, he had never killed a human being. This was a battle between an inexperienced shepherd and an enemy who may have been the most experienced warrior the Philistines had.

Another contrast indicated in the text between Goliath and David was the intimidation factor. Goliath had been intimidating the Israelites for forty days before David arrived. It is significant that David's brothers were among those Israelites who were too chicken to fight the giant. That probably helps explain their anger when they discover David there. The contrast to David is striking. His own brothers mocked him; Saul pointed out that his physical stature was unimpressive; and Goliath seemed to laugh at the thought of what appeared to him to be a child coming out to fight him. The battle pitted the man who caused fear against the unimpressive looking fighter.

Scripture also points out an interesting distinction between the armor the Goliath wore and David's battle attire. Goliath was fully clothed with armor covering his head, chest, waist, and legs. David tried to put on borrowed armor from King Saul, who was likely much taller, but David refused to wear the armor as it was "untested" (1 Sam. 17:39). Instead, David wore to battle what he wore to the battlefield for the purpose of taking his brothers some lunch. David was completely vulnerable. The giant was almost totally covered in armor. Imagine the precision required of David, using a slingshot, to strike a much taller target from a distance while running and hit a man who was protected by an armor bearer in front, carrying a shield, holding a weapon, and wearing a helmet! Although his enemy was over nine feet tall, the actual exposed space at which David had to aim couldn't have been much more than one inch!

Additionally, the Bible indicates a striking difference in the weapons used by the giant and David. Goliath is described as carrying "a sword, a spear, and a javelin" (1 Sam. 17:45) while David carried a stick and a rock! Not exactly a fair fight. David didn't even have a sword. He had a slingshot and a few rocks -- five to be exact. David didn't expect to use or need five stones on Goliath, but, at the brook David remembered this big guy had four sons (Cf. 2 Sam. 21:16-22).

Despite being overwhelmingly overmatched, the young, cute, shepherd boy with a slingshot and some rocks threatened the fully-armored giant, "I'm going to cut off your head, and I'm going to use your sword to do it." This was a battle between a fully-armed, seasoned warrior and a virtually unarmed, inexperienced youth. But, it was the weaponless David who delivered a theology lesson to the giant, "You come against me with a sword, a spear, and a javelin, but I come against you in the name of the Lord almighty, the God of the armies of Israel, whom you have defied. This day the Lord will hand you over to me" (1 Sam. 17:45-46).

One final contrast between Goliath and David was the presence of the armor- bearer. Goliath wasn't alone. He had an assistant. The primary job of the armor-bearer was to stand in front of his master, covering him with a shield to deflect arrows or rocks. So, not only is David fighting a much taller, more experienced, and better armed opponent; he is outnumbered two-to-one. What's interesting is that after David strikes the giant with a rock, we don't hear any more about the armor-bearer. The armed armor-bearer seems nowhere in sight when David approached the giant with a rock in his head, who wasn't yet dead.

Consider the ridiculousness of Saul's desperation. How frantic King Saul must have been to allow David to face the giant. Remember, the country represented by the loser of the battle had to serve the country represented by the winner. So, not only is David's life in danger, but so is the life of the entire country. But, there hadn't been any other takers for more than a month. And, everything was stacked against David. He was outnumbered: the enemy had more experience, better weapons, a reputation, and a track record of intimidation. Maybe you have felt that way before going into a spiritual battle. Peter said that your enemy is like a roaring lion (1 Peter 5:8). Sometimes, he may be like a taunting giant. But, David knew something that you and I need to remember. David said, "The Lord who has always been with me will deliver me from the hand of this Philistine" (1 Sam. 17:37). God is able to deliver you too.

David didn't come looking for a fight; he didn't wear body armor, but he never wavered in faith. Even on the battlefield, David taunted the Philistine, and promised his death and beheading. Then, when the time came for battle, David ran toward the enemy. He ran to the battle line, then ran again to finish Goliath off. This was followed by the Philistines running from the Israelites (cf. 1 Sam. 17:48, 51-52).

What's even more interesting about the story is Saul's apparent unawareness of who David even was. The Bible records that as David was "going out against the Philistine, [Saul] said to Abner the commander of the army, 'Abner, whose son is this young man?'" Saul is entrusting the fate of the country and his kingdom to a guy he doesn't even know!

What Was That Guy's Name, Again?

But, this also says something about Saul. Have you ever met someone who, after meeting them, you have a strange feeling that they have forgotten you? Scripture records in 1 Samuel 16:19-23 that David had previously served as an instrumentalist for Saul to sooth the terrors of evil spirits that came upon him. Saul would call for David, who would play his harp, and the evil spirits tormenting the King would depart from him. It seems that Saul forgot that.

Later in the story, although Abner had been instructed by King Saul to find out who David was, he was apparently disobedient or unable to do so. Perhaps he told Saul and the King did not pay attention to him either since, later, Saul interrogates David for himself. Saul asked David, "Whose son are you?" But, this was the young man with whom Saul was willing to entrust the fate of the nation: a man he didn't know -- young, inexperienced, unarmed, with no armor, no armor bearer, and who's only credentials were that he tended his daddy's sheep (which even David's brothers pointed out were only a "few sheep" (1 Sam. 17:28). That's the man of whom the ladies sang. And, it's no wonder. What an impact he made on the nation!

What kind of influence are you having? David was a servant of influence.

A Servant-Leader

Too often, we have the misperception that service and influence don't go together. We want to be the leader. People follow the leader. We even played games to reinforce that trust as children. If you want to get ahead, you've got to be in front.

Jesus said something different. He said that the one who wants to be first must be last, and the one who wants to be served should be a servant. It seems paradoxical, but only because we are looking at it from our perspective. Remember, God's not so concerned about what you can do for Him but what He can do through you.

The Lord found in David a servant of influence. Scripture says of David that the Lord "chose David to be His servant" (Ps. 78:70). God had a special calling for David's life. The people chose Saul, but God chose David. David came to realize God's special calling on his life. When his wife, Saul's daughter, chastised him for worshiping the Lord in a way that made her uncomfortable, David reminder her that God chose him (2 Sam. 6:21); when David prayed to the Lord upon hearing God's promise to him, David acknowledged that God had chosen him (2 Sam. 7:20-21). When Solomon recounted to the people the sovereignty of God at the dedication of the Temple, he reminded the people that God had said, "I have chosen David" (1 Kings 8:16; 2 Chron. 6:6). When the prophet, Ahijah announced

God's judgment on Israel because of Solomon's sin, the Lord promised to show mercy "for the sake of My servant David, whom I chose" (1 Kings 11:34 cf. 11:13, 32). Finally, the Psalmist, Ethan, quoted the promise of God regarding David, "You said, 'I have made a covenant with My chosen, I have sworn to My servant David'" (Ps. 89:3).

David was chosen of God. But, Scripture often reminds us that we are also among God's chosen.[33] That means, that since God has chosen you, God can do through you what He did through David. If you are His chosen one and you want to be a servant of influence, God needs to find in you what He found in David. Consider what the Bible says God found in David. He first found a servant who was willing to be strengthened by God. Remember David and the giant? David knew (and so did everyone else) that he wouldn't defeat that giant in his own strength. That's why he didn't challenge him to an arm-wrestling match. But, the Lord said that He would strengthen David. That's why the enemy wouldn't outwit him, or wickedness wouldn't afflict him, or plagues wouldn't affect him (Ps. 89:21-23). It's because the Lord would strengthen him.

If you're trying to defeat your giants in your own strength, you're fighting a losing battle. There are some big giants out there. Some of you are facing giants of finance. Others are facing giants of sin and guilt. Maybe your giant is a feeling of inadequacy or a fear of failure.

Whatever giants you may be facing today, the Bible promises that you don't have to face your giant alone. God has promised to strengthen you. Maybe you need to trust Him.

Not only did David trust God for his strength, but He was willing to be a blessing to others. He was a servant who was willing to be used by God to make a difference. That's why the Scripture says that his horn would be exalted. The horn to which God was referring was David's offspring, his heritage.

Let me ask you a question, what kind of difference are you making in your family; in those who come after you? David's family was blessed because it bore God's name. I hope the same can be said of your's and mine. Don't miss why God blessed David and his family. He tells us in the text. The Lord said of David (and ultimately of the Messiah born through his line), "He shall cry to Me, 'You are my Father, My God, and the rock of my salvation'" (Ps. 89:26).

God was looking for a man who would be His. The Lord Himself pointed out the intimacy of their relationship. He was David's Father, God, and sure salvation. The only way that you can have the kind of influence that God wants you to have is by having an intimate relationship with Him. God wants to find in you a heart that's His. That's how your life will make a difference.

Lives David Influenced

Because David was a man of influence, God used his life to touch many other lives. There are three men in particular whose lives were impacted by David. They represent the impact that all our lives need to have for God. The three men are Ittai, Hushai, and Barzillai.

The story of Ittai (2 Sam. 15:19-22) is reminiscent of the story of Ruth. The same level of loyalty that Ruth showed to her mother-in-law, Naomi, Ittai showed to David. It would have been perfectly understandable if Ittai didn't follow David. In fact, even David commented on the irrationality of Ittai's faith. But, Ittai was committed to David. The context of Ittai's story was one of the lowest moments in David's life. His own son, Absalom, had led a revolt against him. This was part of a much larger account in David's life that was marked by consequences of his sin. When Ittai enters the story, David is fleeing Jerusalem. Ittai has no reason to follow David. The text indicates that he only came the day before David was leaving, and he wasn't even a Hebrew. Ironically, Ittai was a Gittite. Now, Gittites were inhabitants of Gath. Remember Gath? That's where Goliath was from. That's where David twice fled. Those are the people who were perennially in battle with Israel. I wonder if Ittai grew up hearing the stories of David killing Goliath? Perhaps, he even met David when David was fleeing from Saul and hiding in Philistine territory. That was certainly not the high point of David's life. Is it possible that Ittai was influenced by David for good when David was not living his most faithful moment? It might be that Ittai was convinced that David was the rightful King of Israel and wanted to be a part of something that he had only heard about. Has anyone ever wanted what you have in your relationship with God simply because of what they heard about you?

Regardless of how Ittai came to Jerusalem, he was there and he was committed. When David objected and offered Ittai a no-shame excuse to go home or stay with Absalom, Ittai responded, "As the LORD lives, and as my lord the king lives, surely in whatever place my lord the king shall be, whether in death or life, even there also your servant will be" (2 Sam. 15:21). Ittai represents the positive influence that David had on someone who came after him. What about you? Is there someone on whose life your life is having an impact? Paul similarly instructed the young man he was mentoring, Timothy, "The things that you have heard from me among many witnesses, commit these to faithful men who will be able to teach others also" (2 Tim. 2:2). In whom are you investing?

Another man in David's life that highlighted his influence was Hushai. David's relationship with Hushai is unique. They are friends (2 Sam. 15:32-37; 2 Sam 16:16; 17:15-16; 1 Chron. 27:33). In fact, Hushai is twice in the text described as David's friend (2 Sam. 15:37; 16:17). David probably didn't have too many friends, especially at this point in his life. Only two other people were ever described as David's friends. One was dead, Jonathan (1 Sam. 18:1), and the other, Hiram (1 Kings 5:1), lived out of the country. It is not entirely clear that they had even met at this point. But, Hushai was more than just a friend; he was probably a confidant. Hushai's job was an advisor. Though the Bible doesn't present him as that for David, no doubt, Hushai was someone in whom David could confide -- someone who would listen and give advice.

David would eventually test Hushai's friendship. He asked Hushai to be a double agent on his behalf. David knew that while he was on the run, a counselor could only do so much. However, if Hushai were to go to Absalom and pretend to be Absalom's counselor, he might be able to undermine the counsel that Absalom received from his other advisors. Moreover, Hushai could report to David what Absalom was planning to do. That's what David asked of his friend (2 Sam. 15:33-36). Hushai proved to be a good friend and an effective secret agent. After gaining Absalom's trust, Hushai began to look for an opportunity to undermine the advice Absalom was receiving. When the moment came, Hushai took full advantage. He gave the King poor advice that sounded wise. Then, he sent word to David of Absalom's next move and potentially saved David's life (2 Sam. 17:1-20).

Have you ever had a friend who would risk his life for you? It's one thing to talk about being a friend but a much different thing to actually live it out. Hushai was

David's friend. He represented the impact that David had on someone who walked alongside of him.

There's a third man in the story whose life demonstrated the impact David had made on him. His name was Barzillai (2 Sam. 17:27-29; 19:31-39). When Barzillai is first mentioned in the story, he is eighty years old. The Bible doesn't say how he and David met. It just says that Barzillai was from Gilead. Gilead was the place where Saul was anointed King (1 Sam. 11:14-15). It was also the location where Abner led the northern kingdom to affirm David as their King. Whether or not Barzillai had supported Saul in the struggle between Saul and David is not known; what is clear is that in the struggle between David and Absalom, Barzillai supported David. Even in peril of his own life, he supported the rightful King.

When David and his men were fleeing from Absalom who was pursuing him with an army, David and his men went to a place called "Mahanaim." There, Barzillai and others came to David and provided them with food and supplies. They had probably left the palace in haste, so Barzillai brought them bedding, bowls, and pottery. David and his men were tired and hungry, so Barzillai brought them dinner and snacks. David and his men were refreshed because they had become "hungry and weary and thirsty in the wilderness" (2 Sam. 17:27-29). David must have been more than just physically refreshed. David wouldn't forget this faithful gesture.

These three relationships of David with Ittai,

Hushai, and Barzillai represent three relationships that ought to be part of your life. Notice, there was someone who came behind David (an apprentice), someone who served with David (a peer), and someone who had gone before David (a mentor). It's been said that those are the three relationships that ought to be a part of every man's life.[34] Are these relationships a part of your life? All of us need someone who has gone before us to show us the way, someone who walks alongside of us to walk with us, and someone who is coming behind us in whom we can invest. In other words, you need to find a mentor; you need to be a mentor; and, you need a friend. David was fortunate to have all three. Every man of God needs friends like that. Every pastor needs men around him like that.

How to Be a Positive Influence on Others for Christ

What kind of influence is your life making for Christ? Influence can be positive or negative. Simply by virtue of his increasing responsibilities, David was going to have an influence on the nation of Israel. Even Saul had an influence on people. The difference was that David was a positive influence on people.

The Bible records a series of events in 1 Samuel 18 that exemplify lessons all of us need to learn on how to be a positive influence on others for the cause of Christ.

Anyone who wants to move from having an influence to making a positive difference in the lives of others needs to follow David's example.

The first lesson that we learn from David in this pericope is that we must genuinely care for people. Saul tended to use people. David cared for them. The best example is found in David's relationship with Saul's son, Jonathan. The Bible tells us that David and Jonathan were best friends.

My wife and I have twin boys. One of the great things about having children is the process of selecting a name for your child. As Christians, we wanted to choose names for our children that reflected the godly heritage of our faith and the hope we had for our children. Our first two boys (who came one at a time) were named one from the Old Testament (Joshua) and one from the New Testament (Timothy). However, naming twins is different. There are many great names in the Bible. Waylon Moore stated that there are 2700 names of men and women in Scripture.[35] However, what my wife and I discovered is that there are not a lot of good names for twins! There is Jacob and Esau. But, who wants to go through life as Esau? There were the twins, Perez and Zerah, who were born of Jacob through daughter-in-law Tamar. Their names mean "dawning" and "breach" -- not exactly what we were looking for. The Bible tells us that Thomas, the Disciple, was a twin. But, we don't know the name of his brother. We did name one of the twins Thomas as a middle name. There is another set of brothers. I think they are twins. The Bible doesn't really say. Their names are Uz and Buz (Gen. 22:21). Can you think of better names for twins than that?! Shockingly, my wife vetoed those names. In the end, we settled on Jonathan and David because we want our boys to exemplify the relationship of these two great men in the Bible. We want them to be best friends.

The Bible uses very descriptive language to describe the relationship between these two men. It tells us that "the soul of Jonathan was knit to the soul of David" (18:1). The word translated "knit" means "tied together" or "bound." These two men were bound together. Verse three declares that they made a covenant of faithfulness together, but, even before that, they had a very special relationship.

This relationship tells us a lot about Jonathan. He was next in line to become King. Under normal circumstances, he would succeed his father, Saul, on the throne. He knew that David was a threat to his and his father's dynasty. But, he loved David. He loved him as himself. He took off his royal robe and gave it to David along with his armor, sword, belt, and bow. There is rich symbolism in Jonathan's removing his royal robe and giving it to David. He is saying to him, "You can have my place."

Later, when David was fleeing from the presence of his father, Saul, Jonathan came to David while he was hiding and encouraged him in the Lord (1 Sam. 23:16). This was a timely encouraging word. David, at this point, was no doubt weary from running for his life and, perhaps, feeling guilty over the consequences of his poor decisions in the situation with Ahimelech. David needed encouaragement. That's what friends do. David and Jonathan were friends. At Jonathan's funeral, David sang a dirge to him in which he bemoaned, "I am distressed for you, my brother Jonathan; You have been very pleasant to me; Your love to me was wonderful, Surpassing the love of women" (2 Sam. 1:26). Do you want to have a good influence on people? Then, you need to learn to care for people genuinely.

The second lesson that we learn from David in this passage about being a good influence is to "behave in front of people wisely." There's a description of David that occurs four times in this pericope (1 Sam. 18:5, 14, 15, 30). This description is only used of four other individuals in Scripture.[36] The writer of Chronicles uses the same word to describe David (2 Chron. 2:12). It is also a description used of the Messiah in Isaiah 52:13.

This word, sakal, is rendered a couple ways among the English translations. The NASV in 1 Samuel 18 translates it "prospered." That is one translation of that Hebrew word. The KJV and NKJV render this word "behaved wisely." This is a better rendering of the word in this context. Saul is not afraid of David because David acquired wealth. Saul is afraid of David because David made good decisions -- decisions that honored God. People could tell a difference in the way that David behaved. Verse 14 states that "David behaved wisely in all his ways and the Lord was with Him." That's what gave Saul cause for fear. David demonstrated himself as a man of insight and understanding. Jesus gave similar instructions to His disciples. He told them as He sent them out to act "shrewdly" (Matt. 10:16). The disciples would learn, as David did, that not everyone is out for your good.

Saul was so cunning, he attempted to trap David by offering him his daughters in marriage (insert your own joke here). Your enemy is cunning. That's why Paul admonished us to put on the whole armor of God to be able to stand against the wiles of the Devil (Eph. 6:11). David, perhaps, remembering the events of this time in his life, would later record in Psalm 14:2 that the Lord looks down from heaven and is looking for someone who behaves wisely. Is that you? If you want to have a positive influence on others, learn to behave with wisdom.

A third lesson that we learn from David in this text is to serve with people faithfully. David was a faithful servant. Wherever Saul sent him, David went. Whatever Saul instructed him to do, David did. Ironically, the only people who ever questioned David's faithfulness were the Philistines, and even that was more of a sign of David's faithfulness to Israel than his disloyalty to them. When the Philistines refused to allow David to fight with them, they remembered how God had already used David and suspected that he would prove more loyal to his own people than he would to the enemy. I hope your enemy believes the same of you.

Saul came to trust David so much that he set him over his army (1 Sam. 19:5). David was his military commander. This was quite a promotion from his previous position as Saul's armor-bearer (16:21). When Saul promoted David, it pleased all the people because they knew that David was faithful. They knew that Saul had made a good choice. The Bible literally says that the selection of David made the people and Saul's servants "glad." But, this was a short-lived promotion. Verse 13 says that once Saul became jealous and fearful of David (and was unsuccessful in killing him), he sent him away from the palace and made him a commander over a unit of a thousand of his forces (13). Now, however you slice it, this is a demotion. David went from being the commander over the whole army to being the leader of a relatively small unit within the army he once led. That would make most of us angry. But, we don't find any indication of that in David in this text.

Like Joseph in Genesis 39, everywhere that David went, the Lord brought success. David was successful militarily. He was successful socially. But, despite all of his success, he was still a faithful servant. Even after Saul twice tried to kill him with a spear (one wonders how Saul had the chance to get off the second throw?), twice tried to cause him to stumble by giving him one of his daughters for a wife, and finally tried to get the Philistines to finish him off (25), David continued to serve the king. When people look at your life, do they recognize your faithfulness in service?

A fourth lesson we learn from David's example in 1 Samuel 18 is to display before people an attitude of humility. Despite all of the great things that this passage records were happening in David's life, he displays remarkable humility. When David was first approached with the possibility of becoming the King's son-in-law, his response was, "Who am I and what *is* my life *or* my father's family in Israel, that I should be son-in-law to the king?" (18) Later, upon being offered the same status a second time by Saul's servants, David similarly responds by referring to himself as a man who was poor and lightly esteemed (23). Don't forget what the passage has already said about him. We are told that everybody was pleased by him (5): women sang songs about him (7); people noticed that things going well for him (15); everybody loved him (16); and even the King's daughter loved him (20). That's hardly the picture of a man who is lightly esteemed. This is not false piety for Saul's benefit, nor is it a man with a poor self-esteem. Remember, he's talking to the servants when he said those things about himself. There's no one there to impress. It's simply the picture of a man with a healthy perspective. He knows who he is. He doesn't get too high when things are going great. On the other hand, he doesn't despair when difficulties come.

Humility isn't pretending to be something that you're not or saying things that you don't believe about yourself in hopes that others will. Genuine humility is understanding and accepting who you are before God. If you are humble, you won't have to tell people about it. They'll know. Besides, if you tell them, it might be an indication that you really aren't what you are claiming to be.

A final lesson that we learn from David in this chapter is to demonstrate to people a character of piety. David was God's blessing on display. Three times in this passage, the Bible tells us that the Lord was with David (12, 14, 28). In fact, even Saul noticed that. When the evil spirits began oppressing Saul, he sought David because he knew David was possessed by the Holy Spirit. But, it was a mixed blessing for Saul. David was able to play his music and soothe the evil spirits within Saul, but the contrast between Saul's heart and David's became too great for Saul to bear. That's why Saul tried to kill him and why the text indicates that he was afraid of David (12).

Despite all the accolades and promotions, David knew from where his blessings came. He didn't try to take the credit for himself. He knew better. Just as everyone else knew that the Lord had blessed David, so also did David. And, David reserved the honor for the Lord. Sadly, too often in our lives, God gets the blame for the bad things that happen, and we take the credit for the good. Just the opposite is usually true. Often the difficult things that we face in our lives are consequences of our sin or poor decisions. Moreover, the good that happens that we are so often tempted to steal the credit for is most often, instead, a testament to God's grace rather than our skill. Do you remember from where your blessings come? James reminded us that every good thing in our lives is a gift to us from God (James 1:17). Don't ever take credit for what God has done. When God blesses you, do you bless Him?

David cared for people; he behaved wisely; he was a faithful servant; he was humble; and he gave God the glory for it all. Do those attributes describe your life? If you want to be a positive influence, follow David's example. Notice how the Bible describes the positive influence David had on those around him. First, David was a positive influence on Saul. Saul noticed David (2), saw how he was faithful (5), and recognized the hand of the Lord in David's life (12). Second, David was a positive influence on Saul's son, Jonathan. Jonathan, because of his love for David, was willing to abdicate the throne for David. Third, David was a positive influence on Saul's supporters (7). The women, who once praised Saul, now praised David. Perhaps, they saw the contrast between the two. To be sure, they knew David had made a more significant impact on the nation that Saul. Fourth, David had a positive impact on Saul's subjects (16). The Bible indicates that "all Israel and Judah" loved David. The people under Saul's domain loved David more.[37] Fifth, David had a positive impact on Saul's servants (24). The servants, who twice brought news to David of the King's offer to marry his daughter, were impressed by David's humble attitude in response.

They even brought back words of praise for David to the King. Finally, David had a positive impact on Saul's daughter, Michal (28). The text doesn't say how Michal knew David. Surely, she had seen him around the palace. Undoubtedly, she had heard of his exploits and what everyone else was saying about him. She probably even knew about the special relationship between her brother, Jonathan, and David. Somehow in the story, her admiration toward David turned to affection. She, like all Israel, loved David. In fact, it is after Saul recognized that Michal loved David, foiling the King's plan to bring trouble in David's life, that Scripture records a second time that Saul was afraid of David. David had a very significant impact in Saul's life and the lives of everyone around the King. How many lives are you impacting for good?

Becoming the Man God Is Seeking

Everyone knows that David was a giant-killer. But, did you know that David influenced others to be giant-killers? Remember when David was preparing to fight Goliath and he went to the stream and found five smooth rocks? He only needed one for Goliath, but the giant had four brothers. We weren't told in that text about those brothers, but David would encounter them later. But, this time, David had help. And, it was a good thing.

The Bible records, in 2 Samuel 21, that there were at least four other giant-killers who were influenced by David. The first was his nephew, Abishai. The day came when the Israelites were again fighting the Philistines. David was fighting with his men. However, David had grown weary in the battle. There was an enemy lurking and hunting David, but he didn't know it. The man hunting David's life was named, "Ishbi-benob." In fact, that probably wasn't really his name but more of a description. The Hebrew rendering of that is "the one who dwells in Nob." Nothing more needed to be said. He was the big guy from Nob. Oh, and the Bible tells us that he was a descendant of the giant, Goliath. But, Ishbi-benob wasn't fighting while everybody else was fighting. He was looking for David. The writer tells us that he was "bearing a new sword [and] thought he could kill David" (2 Sam. 21:16). That's just like your enemy? He's looking for you. He's bringing a new sword. The enemy won't attack you using the same weapons that he always has. He has a new weapon each time to try to kill you. But, David didn't see him coming. Not only that, the Bible says that David was weary. The literal Hebrew word describing how David felt sounds a lot like what it describes. The word is "Uwph." Have you ever felt that way? Your energy is gone. You're tired from the battle. You just feel like "Uwph!" And that's when the enemy attacks. But, David had a helper that day. Abishai saw the giant and killed him before the big guy from Nob could kill his uncle, the King.

That same passage also describes three other giant-killers who were influenced by David. I wish we knew more about Sibbecai, the Hushathite, who was a giant-killer like David and killed Saph, who was a descendant of Goliath (18). Or, wouldn't you like to know more about Elhanan, the son of Jaare-oregim, who struck down another giant from Gath named Goliath?[38] That giant was probably named after his father. Or, how about Jonathan, another nephew of David, who smote a giant from Gath who had six fingers on each hand, six toes on each foot, and was of "great stature" (20-21).

David made a difference in the lives of everyone around him; even those who didn't like him. How about you? Are people different in a good way because of you? It's no wonder that all of the Kings of Judah were later evaluated with David as the standard. He set the bar high. If you want to be a man after God's heart, you've got to have a positive influence in people's lives.

A Man After God's Heart Is Consumed by God's Vision

5

There's a man in the reign of David who is simply an enigma to me. It is Joab. Joab was David's nephew. He is often described as the son of Zeruiah, who was David's sister. His two brothers, Asahel and Abishai, and he were among David's military elite. All three of them were among David's elite forces, his thirty, mighty men (2 Sam. 8:16; 23: 18, 24). Joab was David's commander in chief.

The Bible has some very impressive things to say about Joab. One of the first things we learn about Joab is that he was brave. When David and his men were securing Jerusalem as his capital city early in David's reign, David announced that whoever would attack and kill one of the enemy forces would be his commander. Joab went out first, and that's how he got his job. Joab would prove to be an effective military general. He effectively and skillfully led David's troops in battle (1 Chron. 11:6-8; 2 Sam. 3:22; 10:7-14; 11:1-25; 12:26-29.

Joab was loyal to David as his commander. After defeating the Ammonites at Rabbah and conquering the royal city, he called for David, who was noticeably not with his forces. Joab told David that he had captured the city and gave David the opportunity to receive the credit for the victory. Thus, while David was committing sin with Bathsheba, Joab was winning victories for the King (2 Sam. 12:26-29; cf. 11:1).

Joab also proved to be perceptive. When David was reluctant to bring Absalom back to Jerusalem after Absalom was banished for killing his brother, Joab perceived that David wanted to bring his son back (14:1). He then concocted a creative ruse with a wise woman of Tekoa to trick the King into seeing the error in his reluctance to reunite with Absalom. The plan worked perfectly (14:2-33).

Later, in the Absalom story, after Joab led David's forces to regain the kingdom for David, Joab provided wise counsel for the King after the battle. David was so grieved over the death of Absalom in the battle that he was discouraging the very soldiers that won the battle on his behalf. Joab instructed David to speak encouraging words to his troops or, otherwise, they might leave him. David did as Joab instructed him.

When forces opposed David, Joab supported him. Joab supported David in the revolt of Absalom (2 Samuel 15) and, also, in the revolt of Sheba (2 Samuel 20). Even when David was fleeing the capital from his son, Absalom, Joab remained faithful to his King.

Joab also provided the King wise counsel when David was considering conducting a census. Joab reminded David that the Lord had blessed him and that he did not need to foolishly incur God's wrath by taking a census. Moreover, even when David overruled Joab and commanded Joab to number the people, Joab did as he was commanded (2 Sam. 24:4), despite the fact that the order was "abhorrent" to him (1 Chron. 21:6). So, Joab proved to be discerning and obedient.

In addition, Joab was a giver. The Bible recorded that Joab gave money to the treasury (1 Chron. 26:28). The fact that Joab was among those who were singled out for his gift suggests that his was a substantial gift to the Lord.

Joab was a successful military hero, a perceptive advisor, a loyal servant, and a faithful giver. That sounds like the ideal servant, doesn't it? But wait, there's more.

Joab didn't always follow orders. In the battle with Absalom's forces when the battle began to turn against Absalom's, he fled the city and got his long hair caught in a tree. David had instructed his soldiers to be kind to Absalom; so, even when they found him, they refused to kill him. Instead, they informed Joab. Joab mercilessly killed him (2 Sam. 18:14). Joab was also a murderer. On two occasions, Joab killed men that he perceived as rivals for his position as military commander (2 Sam. 3:26; 20:8-10). Solomon would later comment that Joab killed two men who were "more righteous than he" (1 Kings 2:32). Joab's final act proved to be a fatal error in judgment. When Adonijah attempted to revolt against David and declared himself King, Joab sided with Adonijah (1 Kings 1:7, 19). Perhaps Joab thought he was doing what was right. Or, maybe he was frustrated at David's failure to announce his successor. Either way, he rebelled against David, and it would later cost him his life. When David was giving instructions to Solomon just before his death, one of requests that he made of his son was to execute Joab. David had earlier said of Joab and his brothers, "I *am* weak today, though anointed King; and these men, the sons of Zeruiah, *are* too harsh for me. The LORD shall repay the evildoer according to his wickedness" (2 Sam. 3:39). What David was unable to accomplish in his reign, he trusted Solomon to fulfill in his.

The last picture of Joab in Scripture is the scene of his death. It's a sad and weak denouement to an otherwise exciting and powerful life. The Bible records in 1 Kings 2:28, "Then news came to Joab, for Joab had defected to Adonijah, though he had not defected to Absalom. So Joab fled to the tabernacle of the Lord, and took hold of the horns of the altar." He fled to the altar of the tabernacle thinking that surely, they wouldn't execute him there. He was wrong. Solomon sent Benaiah, another lion-killer to finish what David, an earlier lion-killer, couldn't. There's a sad hint in the verse above. It's almost as if you can hear Joab protesting, "But I was loyal to David. I supported him when Absalom tried to steal the kingdom from him. When others left him, I was there." Indeed he was. But, with Joab you are never quite sure if he is loyal to David or is opportunistic for

Joab. Maybe he was both. Either way, the end is the same

The story of Joab is a story of a man who could see what was in front of him but tended to miss what was beyond. He lacked the vision of God's kingdom that was beyond that of David's. I think Joab genuinely wanted to do right; he just wasn't always sure why he was doing it or what it was all for. He served the King. He supported the King. He gave to the work of the King's kingdom. But, he lacked the vision to see the kingdom that was much bigger than the King. Does any of that sound familiar in anyone you know? Maybe it is true of you.

Did you know that you can work for the Lord, speak well of the Lord, attend the Lord's functions, even give to the Lord, and not follow Him? Jesus said that

God wants more than just your want to. He wants your heart!

at judgment, there will be those who cry out to Him, "Lord, Lord, have we not prophesied in Your name, cast out demons in Your name, and done many wonders in Your name? And then I will declare to them, 'I never knew you; depart from Me, you who practice lawlessness.'" (Matt. 7:22-23)

I'm certainly not saying don't work for the Lord. That's important. Nor, am I saying that the Lord won't appreciate the sacrifices that you make for His work.

What I'm saying is that God wants more than just your want-to. He wants your heart! As much as anyone ever did, David understood that. He didn't always get it right. But, his heart was in tune with the heart of God. That was the final message that David attempted to teach his young son, Solomon. He instructed his son that God, who tries the heart, is delighted with righteousness and integrity (1 Chron. 29:17). Thus, as David was preparing to die, as he was passing the mantle of leadership to his son, Solomon, he wasn't content to just hope his wise son would get it right. He wanted to try to make sure. Some of the final words that David spoke were words of vision to Solomon. He said to the new King,

As for you, my son Solomon, know the God of you father, and serve Him with a loyal heart and with a willing mind; for the Lord searches all hearts and understands all the intent of the thoughts. If you seek Him, He will be found by you; but if you forsake him, He will cast you off forever. Consider now, for the Lord has chosen you to build a house for the sanctuary; be strong; and do it (1 Chron. 28:9-10).

In this charge to his son, David used language that was reminiscent of his own "calling." He told him that "the Lord has chosen you." David was remembering the promise that the Lord made to him in 2 Samuel 7:12 of a son who would reign after him. He wanted his son to get it right. David told him, "Don't take your eyes off of the Lord. He has chosen you for a great task. If you follow Him, He will always lead you in the right direction.

But if you stop following Him, you're in trouble." No more prophetic words could be spoken. That's precisely the picture of Solomon's life. When Solomon was seeking the Lord, his kingdom was secure, and his wealth, wisdom, and works were without equal. But, when he stopped seeking the Lord, trouble came upon Solomon from many directions.

This same pattern was reproduced in the life of Solomon's son, Rehoboam. It is interesting that while the Bible highlights Rehoboam's foolish decision to listen to bad advice (2 Chron. 10:1-19), it also points out some positive aspects of his reign. For example, he did listen to advice from the Prophet, Shemaiah (11:2-4), he acted wisely in securing the borders of his kingdom (2 Chron. 11:23), God allowed him to become strong and established (12:1), and he was visited again by the Prophet, Shemaiah, and seemed genuinely humbled in 12:6 after being confronted in his sin. Also, as a direct result of his humility, God lessened the threat against Judah and conceded in 12:12 that there was "some good" in Judah. In addition, it does appear from 11:13 that the priests and Levites and others who were faithful to the Lord from "all Israel" followed Rehoboam. However, the end result was a negative evaluation of his reign from the Lord, because he did not "set his heart to seek the Lord" (12:14). In the end, Rehoboam was judged not only because of that one foolish decision. It seems he made a conscious decision not to follow the Lord (12:1-2).[39] God's judgment against him was in

> *The opposite of seeking God isn't ignoring Him; it is turning against Him.*

response to his forsaking the law of the Lord (12:2). The opposite of seeking God isn't ignoring Him, it is turning against Him. Rehoboam turned away from the Lord.

Rehoboam's grandson, Asa, was almost a mirror image of him. While Rehoboam was faithful early largely unfaithful to the Lord for the majority of his reign, Asa was faithful to the Lord for the majority of his reign but became unfaithful during his last few years as King. Asa's faithfulness to the Lord was highlighted by the Chronicler in 2 Chronicles 14-16 which includes nine references to seeking the Lord in the chapters devoted to Asa.[40] Not surprisingly, the Bible indicates one of the key reasons for Asa's successful reign in 1 Kings 15:11: "Asa did what was right in the sight of the Lord, like David his father." This was another strong influence on the future of Judah by a King who sought the Lord.

David's desire to seek the Lord is never more clearly expressed than in Psalm 27:8 when he said, "When You said, 'Seek My face,' my heart said to You, 'Your face, O Lord, I shall seek.'"

This passion of David's life is exemplified in Acts 7:46. Luke recorded that "[David] found favor before God and asked to find a dwelling for the God of Jacob." God was pleased with David because he shared the vision of God's heart. He wanted what God wanted. But, don't miss the significance of David's seeking God's heart in the matter. David "asked" of the Lord. He sought God's heart.

David was King. He could have just started building a temple to the Lord. But, rather than just doing things for God and hoping God would bless them, David asked God what God wanted from him. As a result, David was able to see the vision that God had for His people more clearly. What David saw was a more permanent dwelling place for the Lord. Since their inception as a country, Israel had lived in turmoil. Abraham had wandered through Mesopotamia, Israel, Egypt, and back to Israel.[41] Joseph led them back to Egypt. God supernaturally rescued them from slavery in Egypt, and the Israelites spent the next forty years circumnavigating the desert. Finally, God led them back to the land of Israel only to see them become divided as a country and ultimately taken from it again.

David's desire to provide a permanent dwelling place for the Lord was passionate and persistent. The psalmist recorded the intensity of David's desire,

LORD, remember David *And* all his afflictions; how he swore to the LORD, *And* vowed to the Mighty One of Jacob: "Surely I will not go into the chamber of my house, or go up to the comfort of my bed; I will not give sleep to my eyes *Or* slumber to my eyelids, until I find a place for the LORD, a dwelling place for the Mighty One of Jacob" (Ps. 132:1-5).

Mike Bickle pointed out that, for David, it wasn't enough to simply have a private relationship with the Lord whereby he could seek the Lord by himself and for himself. Instead, David wanted a permanent, visible dwelling place whereby God could demonstrate His power for Israel and all the world to see. In fact, David wanted this so intently that he swore that he would forfeit his own comfort until he was able to see the burden of his heart accomplished.[42]

David expressed this passion of his heart in Psalm 69:9-13. He declared that "zeal for Your House has eaten me up" (9). It became an all-encompassing burden for him. He admitted that others didn't understand it (9) and mocked him for it (11). But, David stayed strong in his faith and responded to their criticisms with prayer, pleading for God to hear and answer his request (13). David's desire wasn't always shared by others around him or even by his family (cf. Ps. 69:8); but, that never dampened the burden of David's heart to see the vision accomplished that God had given him.[43]

Do you share the passion of David's heart? Do you long to see God bring a spiritual breakthrough in your community, through your church, or in your life? Do you treasure the public worship of the Lord? This was the passion of David and must be the passion of every man who would be a man after God's heart. David sought a permanent place where Israel could meet God in worship. But note, he verse didn't say that he found favor with God *because* he sought the dwelling place.

Rather the text says that David found favor with God and *then* asked God for the privilege of building that place for Him.

A Favorable Response

He found favor and he asked. The verse seems to suggest that one action influenced the other. In other words, because God was pleased with David's heart, He would eventually grant his request. Perhaps, it was this occasion that served as the impetus for the words David wrote, "Delight yourself also in the law of the Lord, and He shall give you the desires of your heart" (Ps. 37:4).

David's request conveys his heart; he had a desire to worship the Lord. But. it also conveys the uniqueness of David in his time. Many others pretended to worship God in David's day. Others gave gifts, sang songs, and read Scripture. But, David wanted more. He wanted to see God a more permanent part of their lives. It seems clear that God desired the place of worship as well. Is it possible that God was waiting for someone to ask? Could that ever been true in your life? The truth of Scripture is that God wants to work in your life even more than you want Him to work. God wants a relationship with you more than you could ever want one with Him.

Up until this point, the Israelites worshipped God in the Tabernacle. The instructions for the Tabernacle began with Moses' encounter with God on Mount Sinai.

That Tabernacle served Israel through the wilderness. When they moved, the Tabernacle went with them. It served them through the period of the judges. Leaders came and went, but the Tabernacle remained a functional part of Israel's worship. It was their identity.

The Tabernacle remained a part of Israel's worship up until the time of David. However, something significant was different about the Tabernacle under David's leadership. The Ark of the Covenant wasn't there. At first, the Ark wasn't there because it had been taken by the Philistines and then foolishly mishandled by David. Later, David brought the Ark of the Covenant to Jerusalem with him but didn't put it in the Tabernacle. The Tabernacle remained in Gibeon. But, the Ark was taken to a special tent that David has erected for it (2 Chron. 1:4). It wasn't that David didn't want the Ark in the Holy of Holies; it was a constant reminder that he was preparing for a more permanent location in which to house the Ark. David found favor with God and shared the vision of God.

It's no coincidence that the blessing of David occurred right after David's plea before God to build Him a Temple. David found favor with Him. But, it wasn't just God with whom David found favor. The Bible says that David found favor with Saul (1 Sam. 16:22). David also found favor with all the people (1 Sam. 18:5). Samuel recorded that David found favor with Saul's servants (1 Sam. 18:5). Moreover, David found favor with Saul's son, Jonathan (1 Sam. 20:3). Even more, David found favor with the Philistine King, Achish (1 Sam 29:6, 9). Most importantly, David found favor with God. It is reminiscent of statements made of both the boy Samuel and Jesus who increased in favor with God and mankind. I wonder if the same could be said of you.

Do You See What I See?

David found favor in God's sight and sought to see what would please Him. A man who has found favor with God will seek the things that bring God glory. David earnestly desired a dwelling place for the Lord. While the request was noble, it was David's ability to see what God desired combined with a heart that pleased Him that brought God's favor. David didn't just see a need; he saw an opportunity to honor God and strengthen Israel's worship of Him. David loved God's House. He wrote in Psalm 122:1, "I was glad when they said to me, 'Let us go into the house of the LORD.'" The Lord, who knows the heart, recognized a genuine desire for God's glory in David's bold request.

There's a difference between a dream and vision. A dream is something that one hopes will occur. It is typically considered the best-case scenario. If everything were to go right, the dream would be fulfilled. Vision, on the other hand, refers not to what one wishes will happen but to what one sees could happen. A dream is wishful thinking; a vision is a look at what is possible.

We hear a lot of talk today about vision. Leadership books abound in any bookstore extolling the virtues of vision. Solomon said it well, "Where there is no vision, the people are unrestrained" (Prov. 29:18 NASB). The KJV translates that verse, "Where there is no vision the people perish." Rick Warren wrote words of the church that may be equally true when he said, "Where there is no vision, people leave for another parish."[44] It is true that a church more than any organization needs a clear vision of how God could use them. But, the vision must come from Him. It's not about what I want for the church, what I want for God, or even what I think God wants. It's about His plan, His purpose, and, yes, His time. In the end, God affirmed David's vision but not his time and not his plan.

Who's Building a House for Whom?

Instead, when God replied to David through the Prophet, "You won't build a house for Me, but I will build a house for you" (1 Chron. 17:1-10). It wasn't that David's desire was wrong. It wasn't that his vision was wrong. David would get to prepare for the building of the Temple. But, someone else would complete it.

God informed David that He had plans for David's life that David could not imagine. God reminded David of his past. He told him, "I took you from the sheepfold ... I have been with you ... I will appoint a place for My people" (17:7-9). David's desire would eventually be accomplished, but God's purpose at this moment was even bigger than David's. More significant than the Temple was the covenant promise that God made of an everlasting kingdom.

God reminded David that he had come from humble means. It was by God's grace that he reigned on the throne. God had taken him from the fields, been with him in the battles, prepared the way for his kingdom, and used him as an agent of His grace to an entire nation. The Psalmist echoed these words in Psalm 78:70, "He also chose David

His servant, and took him from the sheepfolds .... to shepherd Jacob His people, And Israel His inheritance."

Real success in your Christian life won't be based on what you can do for God. It will be based on what God can do through you. David wasn't wrong for his desire to honor God. In fact, God was pleased with his request. Solomon would later recount God's message to David to that effect, "But the LORD said to my father David, 'Whereas it was in your heart to build a temple for My name, you did well that it was in your heart'" (1 Kings 8:18). God was pleased with David's desire for God's honor, and He will be pleased with yours. But, always make sure that you are seeking His plans more than you want to tell Him about yours.

If They Could See What You See ...

Someone has said that vision is seeing what everyone else has seen but thinking what no one else has thought. David was a man with vision. He wanted to build a Temple unto the Lord to honor Him and provide a permanent place of worship for His people. David didn't always get it right, but he left behind a pas-

> *Real success in your Christian life won't be based on what you can do for God. It will be based on what God can do through you.*

sion for genuine worship. Whether it was the music David played, his psalms, his dancing before the ark of the covenant, his hearing the Word of the Lord, or his institution of temple singers into the worshiping community,[45] David's life was about worship. That was the legacy he left behind.

Generations after his death, the Temple was a lasting reminder of the heart of David for genuine worship of the Lord.

Contrast that with the legacy of Saul. First Chronicles 8 records a sad but very telling legacy of Saul through his family. The names of the family of Saul also tell a story. Saul's uncle's name was Baal (1 Chron. 8:30); Saul named one of his sons Esh-Baal (33); and one of his grandsons was named Merib-Baal (34) -- all showing the influence of the Canaanite pagan god Baal.[46] When compared with the names of David's children, a much different picture emerges. David named his children after his faith in the Lord. The name Solomon means "peace;" Adonijah means "My Lord is Yahweh;" Nathan means "he gave;" Amnon means "faithful;" Daniel means "God is my judge;" and Shephatiah means "Yahweh has judged." Their very names tell the story of David's faith.

But, David's faith didn't only impact his children. Generations of the Kings of Judah were impacted by David. Many of the Kings of Judah were compared with David.[47] Some were good like David; others were poor Kings because they were not like David. For example, in 1 Kings 11, the author emphasizes five times that Solomon did not follow the pattern set by his father David (4, 6, 33, 34, and 38). Does your faith have a positive impact on your family?

In 1 Chronicles 12:32 the Chronicler was recounting the number of David's men who were prepared for battle. Among those were the "men of Issachar" who had understanding of the times." Maybe they were naturally discerning men who blessed David's military. It is also possible that the men of Issachar caught the vision of their leader, David, and had a unique perspective on the particular needs of their day. Do you have understanding of your times? Are others positively influenced because of the godly vision that you instill in them? David was a man of infectious vision.

Becoming the Man God Is Seeking

In 2 Samuel 7, the Bible records an occasion when God's vision met David's passion. The passage highlights David's desire to be the man God wanted him to be. The story begins with a request from David to the Prophet, Nathan. David wanted to build a Temple unto the Lord. It would be a permanent dwelling place for the Ark of the Covenant and a place for the people of Israel to worship the Lord.

Nathan initially responds favorably to David's request and gives the King permission to pursue his dream. However, that night, the Lord spoke to Nathan and gave him a message for David. The message was that David would not be the man to build a Temple unto the Lord. One might think that this news would have been disappointing for David. David might have been tempted to doubt himself or his relationship with God. Maybe God doesn't like me? However, the rest of the chapter indicates God's blessing on David and David's response to God's plan. God followed his refusal of David's request with a covenant of promise. Here, God unfolds a plan that was much greater than David could have imagined or understood. God promised to make David's name great and bless his house. He vowed to give the King an enduring kingdom. Moreover, God declared that one of David's descendants would succeed him who would accomplish David's desire to build a Temple unto the Lord.

Upon hearing this news from the Prophet, the Bible says that David went into the presence of the Lord to pray. The posture of the King is noteworthy. David sat in the presence of the Lord. The Hebrew word used perhaps gives a better dimension. The word actually means "to dwell; remain," expressing a continual stay and not a brief encounter. A similar sense is conveyed in Acts 18:11 when Paul "settled" in Corinth for a year-and-a-half. The Greek word used there has the same nuance as the Hebrew word used of David in God's presence, "to sit down and stay for a while." David didn't just drop by; he came into the presence of the Lord and remained there.

When God called Moses up to the top of Mount Sinai to relate to him the Ten Commandments and Israel's covenant responsibilities, He issued the instruction to come up the mountain twice. In the first call, God instructed Moses to bring along with him Aaron, Nadab, and Abihu and the seventy elders of Israel, and He instructed them to worship Him (Exod. 24:1). Later, God called Moses alone to the top of the Mountain. God's instructions to the Prophet were simply, "Come up to Me on the Mountain and remain there" (Exod. 24:12). Moses would be given the tablets of stone and the commandments, which God indicated that He had written. But, his purpose was much more than that. After all, the Bible indicates that God wrote the Ten Commandments, and, really, how long would it take God to write out the Ten Commandments anyway? If God can create the universe in a few days, surely He can write out His commands in a few seconds. So, why was Moses on the mountain for forty days? The answer is in the purpose for which God called him. "Come up the mountain and remain there." Just be with Me. Imagine this: God's wants to be in your presence more than you want to be in His! God desires what we need more than we desire it. Larnelle Harris captured this thought well in his song, "I Miss My Time with You." Isn't it sad that we get so preoccupied with our concerns and the pursuit of what we want that we miss out on the one thing we most need? God wanted that for Moses. David wanted that for himself. When was the last time you spent time "being" in God's presence. Not just passing by – dwelling. That's what Moses did on the mountain, and that's what David did. He made a conscious effort to be where God was; He didn't demand God come to where he was. Then, when he was in the very presence of God, David sat down.

David's words to God indicate the heart of a man after God's heart. The King cried out, "Who am I?" (18) David was humble before the Lord. The King of the greatest nation on earth now sat humbly in the presence of the King of the universe. He knew he wasn't worthy of God's grace. And, he knew how he got where he was. It wasn't because of what David had done. It was because of what God accomplished for him.

When David prays, you hear the heart of a man who trusts and who knows God's promise is much bigger than he understands. In fact, God is much bigger than he could comprehend. All he could say was, "You are great, O Lord God. For there is none like You, nor is there any God besides You" (22). What a vision of a man who's vision was too small! David concludes his prayer with a plea for the confirmation of the words of the Prophet and an expression of praise to God. He prayed with confidence that God would fulfill the promise He had made to David.

But, before you move past the story too quickly, let me point out a couple of thoughts. First, don't miss the impact of the fact that God declined David's request. God said, "No." David probably didn't hear that word very often. But, God rejected his request. Moreover, did you notice that when God declined David's request, He didn't even give a reason why. No explanations -- just no. You do know that God isn't obligated to explain Himself to you, right? Now, in His grace, there are times when God patiently explains Himself and His ways to us. However, more often, He doesn't. He doesn't need a reason and certainly doesn't have to defend Himself to you or me. He is God. David expressed it well, "What more can David say to You?" (20) God would ultimately provide something better, but the answer to David's request was still, "No." The truth is, David's vision wasn't a part of God's perfect plan.

Have you ever been denied something you really wanted? No one likes to hear the word "no," especially from God. David will later twice recount this story -- once to Solomon (1 Chron. 22: 7-10) and, later, to all

Israel (1 Chron. 28:3). In both places, David indicates that the reason that God would not allow David to build a Temple unto Him was because David was a man of war. Apparently, at some point, God revealed to David why he would not be allowed to carry out his dream. Now, David is content to help make his dream possible for someone else to fulfill. God opened up David's eyes to see His vision.

It may be that your dreams and big plans won't all come true. Or, maybe in you'll spend your life preparing for a fulfillment that will come after you are gone. But in God's grace, He gives us the opportunity to see what will be. Maybe, occasionally experiencing God's "no" helps us to see the wonder of God's "yes!"

Ultimately, at the dedication of the Temple, when David's dream finally came true, Solomon reflected on God's promise to his father. He declared before the people assembled to dedicate this wonder, "Now it was in the heart of my father David to build a temple for the name of the LORD God of Israel. But the LORD said to my father David, 'Whereas it was in your heart to build a temple for My name, you did well in that it was in your heart. Nevertheless you shall not build the temple, but your son who will come from your body, he shall build the temple for My name'" (2 Chron. 6:7-9). Solomon declared that his father's heart was right and the Lord's promise was fulfilled.

David found favor, and he asked of God. The text doesn't say that he found favor because he asked. We learn that David found favor and asked. He became what God desired of him and demonstrated it by what he desired from God. He found favor in God's sight. Doesn't that imply that the Lord was looking? Now, David, like Moses, never got to see the completion of the vision that God gave to him (1 Kings. 8:17-18). But, he was a part of preparing the way for God to accomplish His plan.

Never forget, it's not just about you and me. God's plans are much bigger. It might be that His "no" to you today is only laying the groundwork for a much greater "yes" tomorrow. The question is, are you willing to wait on God's timing? Are you willing to continue to be faithful to Him even when things don't work out how you want or when you want? To become who God seeks, you have to want what God wants. Then, you can see the vision that God alone can make possible.

A Man After God's Heart Pursues God's Mission

6

Remember Barzillai? He was David's mentor and friend. He supported David when others were abandoning him. When David tried to honor his aged friend for his faithfulness to the King, Barzillai refused (2 Sam. 17:27-29; 19:31-39). Instead, like a faithful mentor, he demonstrated that there was another man in whose life he was investing. This young man's name was Chimham. It was an act of unselfishness that could easily be overlooked in the story. But, while this was the last appearance of Barzillai in Scripture, this would not be the last we would hear of Chimham.

Some have suggested that Barzillai's refusal of David's offer demonstrated a lack of courage or an illustration of making excuses instead of being faithful.[48] I don't agree. I think Barzillai was a man who was more concerned about others than he was about himself.[49] David is offering Barzillai a comfortable retirement. But, that doesn't seem to be in his character. It is just as likely that Barzillai had other men whose lives he was touching who needed him more than he need the comforts of David's blessings. The name Barzillai means "[man] of iron." This ironman doesn't appear to be the kind of man to quit. It seems more likely that he knows that he has more important uses of his time than retirement.

It may be that David's intention was to bring on Barzillai as a replacement for Ahithophel, who was his great grandfather-in-law and who had been his former advisor. However, Ahithophel abandoned David and defected to Absalom. Perhaps, David's intention was to use Barzillai in some sort of advisory capacity. However, Barzillai did not want to be an added burden to David (19:35) and politely refused, requesting the Kings honor be given to Chimham.[50]

David did as Barzillai requested and more. He promised that "Chimham shall cross over with me and I will do for him what seems good to you" (19:38). Two verses later, the text indicates that David went on to Gilgal, and Chimham accompanied him. In addition, 1 Kings 2:7 indicates that David did not forget Barzillai. He encouraged his son, Solomon, to show kindness to the descendants of Barzillai and even recommended that they be allowed to eat at the King's table because of their kindness to David. The Hebrew text suggests that there were others from Barzillai's family who were with him when he assisted David.[51] In the end, David did for Barzillai and his family what both he and Barzillai wanted.

It would have been understandable if the King only brought Chimham along to appease his older friend. It would have been easy just to put him on the team but

never really treat him like everyone else. After all, he
wasn't really the guy David wanted. David wanted the
older, wiser counselor. What he got was the younger,
otherwise unknown Chimham. If this were the last reference to Chimham in Scripture, we might be left to
wonder how David must have treated Chimham. But,
Scripture preserves one other reference to Chimham that
suggests that David did more than just bring Chimham
on the team. The Bible records in Jeremiah 41:17 a reference to a location bearing the name Chimham. The
town had some sort of inn in which people could stay.
It is that inn that is reference by Jeremiah. It is very
likely that this town was part of the land that was given
to Chimham by David.[52] It's proximity to Bethlehem
would suggest that likelihood. Even more interesting is
the possibility of a much greater significance being given
to Chimham centuries later. Some have suggested that
the inn in Chimham was the location of the birthplace
of Christ.[53] It is clear that David did what he promised,
and it could be that God used David's fulfillment of his
promise as an occasion to fulfill His.

I Have Found David

Among the passages describing what God was looking for and ultimately found in David, we have seen that
David was a man with a heart like God, a servant of
influence, and a leader with vision. There's one other

passage that expresses the result of God's search and selection. It is Acts 13:21-23. The context of the passage is a message by Paul in the synagogue of Antioch. The theme of the message is God's sovereign grace. Paul reminded them that God chose them for His people, provided for them a land to call their own, and established leaders who would guide them. For a moment, Paul pauses in the middle of the story of God's grace to reflect on God's selection of David.

The selection of David as King culminated a divine search. God was looking for something -- for someone. He found that man in David. Paul repeats the words of the Psalmist in Psalm 89:20, "I have found David." It's a curious phrase coming from an omniscient God. It's not like David was lost. Nor, is God somehow surprised by the discovery of the man who would pattern his heart after God's. Instead, Paul puts it into perspective. God found a man who would be obedient to His will and become the agent of fulfillment of the God's promise.

God's promise began long before David. Even before God announced His plan to Samuel, God already knew. God's promise continued through David when God affirmed to his servant that through his lineage would come the Messiah (1 Chron. 17:1-15). During His earthly ministry, Jesus affirmed God's promise through David of Himself in Matthew 22:41-45). Peter, in his sermon at Pentecost, declared that God had fulfilled that promise in Christ and that David prophesied of the Christ's resurrection (Acts 2:30-31) and ascension (2:25). Finally, the Apostle Paul acknowledged God's promise to David fulfilled in Christ, revealed by the resurrection, and confirmed by the Holy Spirit (Rom. 1:1-6).

Indeed, God fulfilled His promise to David. One might ask, "Why David?" Luke records the answer for us when he writes "will do all My will" (Acts 13:22). The bottom line is, David wanted what God wanted. He was willing to do all that God desired to accomplish through him. Is that true of you? Is there anything that God might ask of you that you are unwilling to do?[54]

David did all of God's will. The reader is not left to wonder why God chose David. He gave us the key: David fulfilled God's purpose.[55] That's why God told Solomon that he walked before God like David did, God would establish his throne and kingdom like He promised David He would (2 Chron. 7:17). God wanted Solomon to do His will like David did.

Note that the Bible doesn't say that David always did the will of God. It says that he accomplished all of God's will. He completed the task that God desired of him. How do we learn what God wants? It's not that hard. I'm convinced that too often as believers we fundamentally overcomplicate God's will. Remember, it is God's will. The very words suggest that it is something that God wants you to know. So, if God wants you to know it, doesn't it make sense that He is going to provide a way for you to know His will for your life? The Prophet Micah agreed in Micah 6:8, "He has shown you, O man, what *is* good; And what does the LORD require of you But to do justly, To love mercy, And to walk humbly with your God?" God does have a will and a plan for your life. If you seek Him, He will make it clear to you.

How'd He Do That?

The example of David reveals that the will of God is a doing process on our part. True, God could accomplish His purpose without us. But, He chooses to use us. God highlighted the selection of David as significant because David would DO all

I'm convinced that too often as believers we fundamentally overcomplicate God's will.

that God desired. It is also true that God has a purpose for your life.

David's example teaches us two critical truths about doing the will of God. First, the vision that God has for our lives and His church is bigger than you or me. Don't get it backwards. You and I aren't doing God a favor by serving Him. God has shown you and me His grace by allow us the privilege of serving with Him. All of God's will was not accomplished in David's lifetime. It is true that David accomplished all that God desired from him during his lifetime, but God's plan was much bigger than David. It began long before him and continues to this day long after him.

It's the same with you and me. God is never confined to our small way of thinking. Instead, He sees from an eternal perspective. That means that you and I are custom-made to fit within God's big plan. You weren't an afterthought. God made you like you are for a reason. He wants you to be a man after His heart. You and I need to stop settling for small plans and focus on the bigger mission of God. That's what David did.

David had a heart for the world and not just Judah and Israel. To capture David's heart for the nations, one needs only to look at the psalms that he wrote. David often spoke of God's sovereign love for and rule over all the nations of the world.[56] David declared,

Among the gods *there is* none like You, O Lord; nor *are there any works* like Your works. All nations whom You have made shall come and worship before You, O Lord, and shall glorify Your name. For You *are* great, and do wondrous things; You alone *are* God (Ps. 86:9).

To be obedient to God's command, to fulfill our Lord's commission to take the Gospel to all the world, we need to catch the passion of God's heart. We need a worldwide mission.

The second truth we learn about the will of God is not just that it is beyond the parameters of our small scope, but that, in His grace, God will use you and me to see it accomplished. David didn't get to see the fulfillment of his vision for a Temple, but he did get to see the process started. He didn't get to see God's ultimate fulfillment of a Messiah through his lineage, but God allowed him to see what God would do.

Jesus left us instructions to take the Gospel to Jerusalem, Judea, Samaria, and the whole world. Too often, we've handled that like a multiple choice. We don't get to pick which one of those we choose to pursue. We are called and accountable for all of them. That means that every man of God should be actively participating in mission endeavor that are global. You can pray. You can go. You can give. You can encourage those who do. How could God use you? How is God using you to prepare the next generation to continue to carry out His mission?

Your life has a purpose, and it's bigger than you could imagine! You can spend your life trying to accomplish your plans and, perhaps, be a part of something temporary. Or, you could spend your life serving the bigger purpose that God has for your life and be a part of something eternal. How do you want to spend your life? God has a plan for your life. Your ministry is to spend your life pursuing it.

The epitaph to David's life and ministry reveals a great deal about his life. Paul summarized David's life and God's hand on it in Acts 13:36, "For David, after he had served his own generation by the will of God, fell asleep." Did you catch the significance of that verse? When David fulfilled the purpose that God had for his life, God took him home. The next verse says that David was buried. Peter said in Acts 2:29 that his tomb was still among them. One thing you won't find in Scripture is a funeral for David.

It's a little odd. Normally when a great man or woman died in Scripture, the writer pauses to portray a picture of his or her funeral. But, have you ever noticed that there's not one for David? Peter and Paul mentioned his tomb; 1 Kings 2 mentions that David "slept with his fathers and was buried" (10); and Chronicles tells us that he died of a ripe old age (29:28). But, no one talks about an elaborate burial. It doesn't mean that he didn't have one. It just means that it wasn't important for the story.

Once David fulfilled the purposes of God for his life, God brought him home. It's sort of like the picture of Enoch in Genesis 5. Enoch was described as a man who walked with God. One day, Enoch was walking with God on earth, and, the next day, Enoch was walking with God in heaven. Moses told us that Enoch was no longer because God took him (24). In the end, David accomplished the purposes that God established for his life, and God took him home. Regardless of what kind of ceremony may or may not have accompanied David's death, can you imagine the welcome home he must have received in glory?

In David, the Lord found a man who would accomplish all His will. And, through his descendants, God fulfilled His promise to the world. Paul affirmed, "From this man's seed, according to *the* promise, God raised up for Israel a Savior, Jesus" (Acts 13:23). David had a heart for the world like God's heart. He was willing to be used of God to impact the world.

One last thought about David and his God-ordained mission. Even though the task was huge and unimaginable, did you notice that David never asked how? He never wondered if God would be able to fulfill His plan through David. He just believed that, somehow, God could use him for His purpose.

A Man After God's Heart Carries out the Mission of God's Heart

I believe that God has the same desire for your life and mine. He probably won't use you like He used David. But, if you will trust Him, God will accomplish His purpose through your life and use you to impact the world because that's the heart of God. The only question that remains for you and me to answer is "What is your place and mine in God's mission?" We know what God's mission is for the world. We need to catch hold of God's mission for our lives. I'd like to submit to you that God has a place for you in His service. You may be asking, how can I find my place in God's work? Follow these simple steps and ask yourself these five questions:

P.   What is My **Passion**?

L.   What are My **Liabilities**?

L.   What is My **Ability**?

C.   What is My **Calling**?

E.   What have been My **Experiences**?

The P stands for passion. What is it that you LOVE to do? I mean, what gets you up in the morning? What lights your fire? God has made you unique. You are who you are for a reason. The passions that you have make you who you are. So, what is it that you are most excited about doing? David said if you delight yourself in God and His Word, He will give you the desires (passions) of your heart (Ps. 37:4-5).

The L stands for liabilities. What are the areas in your life that you need to work on? Do you have sin in your life that is keeping you from accomplishing God's purpose and plan for your life? Are there things about you or your personality that would prevent you from accomplishing the tasks that He has for you? David said, "Search me, O God, and know my heart; Try me, and know my anxieties; and see if *there is any* wicked way in me" (Ps. 139:23-24).

The A stands for abilities. What is it that you can do that no one else can? It doesn't mean that you have to have skills that no one else does or abilities that no one else has. That might be true of you. But, even more than that, you have opportunities that match the abilities you have that make you uniquely suited to accomplish what

God desires from you. Indeed, David was a gifted man. He had musical ability. He could take care of sheep. He could handle a weapon. He could influence people. David was the five talent guy that Jesus described in the parable of the talents (Matt. 25:14-30). But, when the master in the parable judged his servants, he did not brag on them because they started with more than someone else. He blessed the servants who were faithful. If God has given you ability, whatever it is, He wants you to use it to His glory. What abilities do you have? Maybe you can build -- you can build for God. Maybe you can sing -- you can sing for God. Can you speak? You could use that ability for His service as a preacher or a teacher. Can you encourage, give, love, share, etc. Those are gifts to you from God. You indeed have "talent on loan from God." Make sure and use it for His glory. That's why He gave it to you.

The C stands for calling. Where do you feel God is calling you right now? Don't complicate the matter by worrying about next year or even next week. What do you believe is God's will for you today? Start there. If you seek Him, He will be found by you. David exemplified this is Psalm 27:8 when he testified, *"When You said,* 'Seek My face,' my heart said to You, "Your face, LORD, I will seek." Later, David would declare, that all who seek His heart will be blessed (Ps. 119:2). When you seek Him, you will find Him. Do you want to know God's will for your life? Seek Him. It is uniquely suited for you and no one else. Jerry Vines said, "There are no carbon copies of God's will."[57] It is unique to you. Indeed, God does have a wonderful plan for your life. If you look to Him, He will make it known to you. God wants you to know His will. If you ask Him, He will reveal it to you.

The E stands for experiences. What experiences has God allowed in your life that could be used for His glory. The Bible affirms that God is able to cause all things to work together for good and for His glory to those who love Him and are called to His purpose (Rom. 8:28). That doesn't mean that everything that has ever happened to you has been good. It does mean that God may use that experience to give you an opportunity to be a blessing to someone else. God has done that in my life. Through some of the most painful experiences of my life, things that I would not want to go through again, God has provided opportunities for me to use them to encourage someone else. God doesn't bring every bad experience into your life. But, God can even use the bad ones for His glory.

What is your PLACE in God's service? Never forget, you are no accident or coincidence. God made you like you are for a reason. His desire is for you to use the abilities and gifts that He has given to you for His glory.[58] God honored David because he was willing to be used by God to accomplish His purpose.

Never forget, you are no accident or coincidence.

God Wants More Than Just Your Want-to

Recently, I was struck by the repeated occurrence of the phrase, "we will do." You see it typically in response to a clear command from the Lord. This phrase is used as a covenant response of God's people to His expectations. It is never more clearly expressed than in Exodus 19:8. The people were assembled before Mt. Sinai. God was about to deliver to them His covenant conditions. As Moses was preparing the people for the encounter, they responded, "All that the Lord has spoken, we will do." It sounded great. It even reads great in the text. But, it wasn't long before the people demonstrated by their disobedience that they didn't really mean what they said.

The same phrase occurs twice in Exodus 24:3, 7, after the giving of the law and the commandments; in Numbers 32:31, as the half tribe of Manasseh and the tribes of Reuben and Gad are being given conditions for faithfulness in their new land; in Joshua 1:16, after the installation of Joshua as the new leader of God's people; in Nehemiah 5:12, after Nehemiah called on the people to repent; and in Jeremiah 42:20, when Jeremiah predicted the Babylonian exile. Each time, the people promised "we will do" what God said. Each time they failed. How many times have you made promises to God that you have failed to keep? The work of the Kingdom of God isn't accomplished by empty promises. Interestingly, the only time the people of Israel actually did what they said when making such a promise to God, was when they were asking permission to live outside of God's will (Num. 32:31)! But, if you want to be used of God to fulfill His purpose and mission, we are going to do more than just SAY we are willing for God to use us; we're going to have to let God use us. Jesus said, "The one who hears My words and does them" is like the man who built his home wisely. On the other hand, Jesus indicated that anyone who does not do according to His words is like the man who built foolishly (Matt. 7:24-27). James reminded us not to simply listen to the Word but to do what is says (James 1:22). David didn't always do God's will, but he did all of God's will. Like Paul, he could say at the end of his life that he had fought the good fight, finished the course, and kept the faith (2 Tim. 4:7). What about you? Are you fulfilling God's desire in your life and through your life? Are you living up to all the great things you always wanted to accomplish for God?

Becoming the Man God Is Seeking

What do you want your last words to be? Consider some of the last words from these famous people:

Adams, John Quincy (1767-1848) "This is the last of earth! I am content."

Addison, Joseph (1672-1719) "See in what peace a Christian can die."

Akiba ben Joseph (c.40-c.135) "The paper burns, but the words fly free." (at the stake, when the Torah was also burned).

Antoinette, Marie (1755-1793) "Farewell, my children, forever. I go to your Father."

Astor, Lady Nancy (1879-1964) "Jakie, is it my birthday or am I dying?" (Seeing all her children assembled at her bedside in her last illness).

Barrymore, John (1882-1942) Die? I should say not, dear fellow. No Barrymore would allow such a conventional thing to happen to him.

Beaverbrook, Lord (1879-1964) "This is my final word. It is time for me to become an apprentice once more. I have not settled in which direction. But somewhere, sometime, soon." (The last public statement before his death, speech at Dorchester Hotel, 25 May 1964).

Becket, Thomas à (c.1119-1179) "I am ready to die for my Lord, that in my blood the Church may obtain liberty and peace."

Beecher, Henry Ward (1813-1887) "Now comes the mystery."

Bogart, Humphrey (1899-1957) "I should never have switched from Scotch to Martinis."

Cleveland, Grover (1837-1908) "I have tried so hard to do the right."

Dickinson, Emily (1830-1886) "... the fog is rising."

Louis XIV (1638-1715) "Why are you weeping? Did you imagine that I was immortal?"

Morgan, John Pierpont (1837-1913) "I've got to get to the top of the hill..."

Raleigh, Sir Walter (1554-1618) "I have a long journey to take, and must bid the company farewell."

Smith, Adam (1723-1790) "I believe we should adjourn this meeting to another place."

Villa, Francisco `Pancho' (1878-1923) "Don't let it end like this. Tell them I said something."

Washington, George (1732-1799) "It is well, I die hard, but I am not afraid to go."

Webster, Daniel (1782-1852) "I still live."

Wilde, Oscar (1854-1900) "Either this wallpaper goes, or I do!"[59]

Maybe your last words won't be immortalized, but it doesn't mean that they won't be heard. When the epitaph of your life is written, what would you like for it to say?

Fortunately, we know what some of the last recorded words of David were. We find them in two different psalms reflecting on two different occasions in 2 Samuel 22 and 23. It's not too surprising that David, the skillful musician, chose music to express some of the final earthly words he would utter. The headings tell us the occasions for the writing of the psalms. The placement at the end of 2 Samuel suggests that David may have repeated them as he neared the end of his life.

In the first Psalm, David is looking back on how God protected him from Saul. David confidently asserted that the Lord was His stronghold. He had always been faithful, and David knew that He always would be (2-4). He remembered that when he called to the Lord, the Lord saved him (4). Even when death seemed very near, the Lord heard him (5-7). In His anger, the Lord brought judgment on His enemies and rescued His servant (8-17). David knew that the Lord rescued him because He delighted in him (20). Finally, David makes a confident and curious claim. He twice declared himself to be clean before the Lord (21, 25). The circumstances of when David wrote this psalm and when he is likely reciting it are dramatically different. Much has happened in the intervening years. Yet, clearly, God had heard and answered David's prayer from Psalm 51 to create in him a clean heart. Now, near his death, David can affirm again that his heart is clean before the Lord. David goes on to extol the Lord's ways as right (31) and His Word as perfect (31); He gave power and skill in battle (35), and brought victory over his enemies (40-41). Finally, David remembered that it was the Lord who established his position as King (44). David knew he had much for which to be thankful to the Lord.

Second Samuel 23:1 indicates that the words of that psalm are the final words of David. Maybe the last words David ever spoke. Imagine David on his deathbed having ordained Solomon as King as he promised, admonished his son to be faithful, and encouraged the people to support the new King. Now, as he draws his feet under the covers one last time, maybe surrounded by the musicians he sanctioned, he prepares to meet the Lord with a song on his lips.

The words of David's last song speak volumes. It reflects the character of a man whose heart sought after God. He had learned from the mistakes of his past and could confidently assert that when one rules with righteousness, "h*e shall be* like the light of the morning *when* the sun rises, A morning without clouds, *Like* the tender grass *springing* out of the earth, By clear shining after rain" (4).

In that moment, David became acutely aware that God's promise to him would live beyond him. He knew that God had made an everlasting covenant with him and that, indeed, God's promises are sure (5). He claimed God at His Word. They may be the last words he ever spoke. They would be how he would be remembered.

What do you want your last words to be? David's last words were words of faith and hope. He was claiming God at His Word and pointed people to His promise. You must know that God will also be faithful to fulfill His Word in your life, too.

David's last words declare to us "look what God has done and what He will do." Indeed, as God was always faithful to David, He will always be faithful to you. David was a man after God's own heart. And you can be, too.

Conclusion

David had a special group of men that I wish we knew more about, and I wish that I were more like. First Chronicles 13 records the list of David's military resources by tribe. Most of the tribes list the number of men equipped and ready for war. However, one of the tribes is different; it is the tribe of Issachar. Rather than listing the men of this tribe who were ready for war, the Bible records that the men of Issachar "had understanding of the times, to know what Israel ought to do, their chiefs were two hundred; and all their brethren were at their command" (1 Chron. 12:32). This verse speaks volumes about this tribe, and there is much more that one might wish they could know about their designation.

First, remember that the whole pericope is about military resources. Some have tried to read into the discretionary abilities of these men some sort of astrological abilities,[60] but that seems highly improbable in the context. Since this section is detailing what resources were available to David, a reference to men among David's men with abilities in divination seems unlikely.

Second, the context of the larger picture is that David is being made King over a united kingdom. After Saul, the kingdom had briefly divided, and, now, David will preside over a reunited kingdom. Thus, the insight that the men of Issachar possessed needs to relate to the two parts of the context: the military resources available to the King and the larger picture of the united kingdom.

It is likely that when the text states that they understood the times, it is indicating that they were committed to facilitating David's coronation as King over both Israel and Judah. They must have understood that the need of their day (times) was a Godly leader like David.[61] Perhaps, one of the greatest needs in our day is men who understand the times and what needs to be done in them.

The other aspect of the men of Issachar that is unique in the passage is that the verse only highlights the chiefs of Issachar, not the actual number of fighting men. One could assume, if the proportion of chiefs to fighting men were the same as it was with Naphtali (cf. vs. 34), that the actual number of fighting men would be 7,400. However, it is also possible that since a different word is used with reference to the chiefs of Issachar than the word used with reference to the captains of Naphtali, that something more significant is being communicated about the tribe of Issachar. It could be that the number of chiefs listed among them is what is being emphasized. They had 200 chiefs. In other words, the Chronicler may be saying that this group of men was so significant there were 200 of them who were capable of being chiefs in David's military. So that, their wisdom and insight was for David the resource, not just the number of available men. This would explain why the tribe is singled out. These men, with all the other tribes listed, came to Hebron "with a loyal heart" to make David their King (12:38).

What we need today are more Issacharian men. We need men who stand out, who are loyal, and who understand our time and what needs to be done about it. More than just names on a role, we need leaders who are willing to make a difference in this world. What leader or pastor wouldn't be greatly blessed by men like that? How do you become Issacharian? Solomon reminded us that a fear of the Lord is the beginning of wisdom (1:7). James tells us that if any of us lacks wisdom, let him ask of God (1:5). Both passages teach that the wisdom that will be needed to make a difference in our world can only come from God. We need to stop looking for the wisdom for our times in all the wrong places. Who's going to be that man of wisdom? If David needed them, we all need them.

The fact that David attracted such great men speaks as much about David as it does about those men. Leaders only follow leaders. It was only one of David's many great qualities. But, not everything about David was always great. In the end, I see in David many attributes that I wish were part of my life and so many others I'm afraid may be.

But it is the four attributes that the Bible points out that God found in David that I want us most to consider. If we want to be men after God's heart, this seems like the best place to begin. We need men who are known by their character. We need men who lead through service. We need men who are consumed by God's vision. We need men who are pursuing God's mission. You can be one of those men.

My purpose in writing this book is not to get you or myself to be more like David. I want us to learn to be more like who David was like. Among the many things that the Bible says about David, we learn that David was a man after God's heart. Something about David's heart was something like something about God's heart. It's easy to think about David in stained glass window concepts. David was a great man. He was good-looking, gifted, strong, and passionate. He was a man's man and a ladies' man.

David was also appropriately named. I can't imagine that his parents could have had any idea the significance of their son's name when they gave it to him. David's name means "beloved." It was perhaps his greatest asset and the cause of one of his greatest failures -- people loved David. Even when David was serving Saul, the people loved David (1 Sam. 18:22). Saul loved David so much that he hated him. Saul's daughter, Michal, loved David. Saul's own servants loved David. Ironically, the one who seemed to have loved David the most, Saul's son, Jonathan, stood the most to lose by loving him.

The people followed David. They were sacrificially committed to him. One day, David was thirsty and simply made a statement, "I wish that I had some water from the well in Bethlehem," his home town. Now, when he said that, David and his forces were engaged in a fierce battle with the Philistines. After David said that, and apparently unknown to David, three of his warriors broke through the enemy camp, traveled to Bethlehem, drew water, carried it back to David, and broke back through the enemy camp to bring it to their leader (1 Chron. 11:17-19). That's how much his men loved him.

The stories of David's mighty men are some of the most amazing stories ever told in human history. David had men who were mighty, fearless, and intensely loyal to him. Jashobeam and Abishai, who both fought 300 men at one time by themselves and won, were among David's mighty men. Benaiah, who killed a lion in a pit on a snowy day and fought an Egyptian giant with only a club in his hand before killing the giant with his own spear, was one of David's mighty men (1 Chron. 11:10-26). Sibbecai, the giant-killer, was one of David's mighty men (2 Sam. 21:18). Elhanan, who killed a giant from Gath named "Goliath," whose spear was like a weaver's beam, was one of David's mighty men.[62] David had such an amazing group of men. Jonathan, who killed a giant from Gath, one of Goliath's sons, who had six fingers on each hand and six toes on each foot, apparently didn't even make the team (2 Sam. 21:21). David had mighty men from Israel, but he also had Harorites, Pelonites, Tekoites, Anathothites, Hushathites, Ahohites, Netophathites, Gebeahites, Pirathonites, Arbathites, Baharumites, Shaalbonites, Gizonites, Hararites, Mecherathites, Carmelites, Ezbaites, Hagrites, Ammonites, Berothites, Ithrites, Hittites, Reubenites, Mthnites, Ashterathites, Aroerites, Tizites, Mahavites, Moabites, and Mezobaites (1 Chron. 11:26-47). In addition, David had Cherethites, Pelethites, and Gittites as his special forces (2 Sam. 15:18). They followed him because they loved him and must have seen in him what they wanted to become.

David was loved by his men. He was also loved by the nation. Even when the kingdom was divided and David ruled in the south and Saul's son, Ish-bosheth, ruled in the north, many of the people from the north defected to the south because they loved David (1 Chron. 12:19). Even when the kingdom was united under David's leadership, the northern tribes and the southern tribes argued over which side had a greater claim to David as King (2 Sam. 19:43). The nation loved David.

Most of all, we learn that the Lord loved David. It would be hard to think of a more appropriate name for him than "beloved." He was the man whom God loved.

David spoke of God's love for him in Psalm 17:8 when he beseeched the Lord to "keep me as the apple of your eye."[63] He knew that the hand of the Lord was upon him.

It was a mutual affection. David loved God. David proclaimed in Psalm 18:1, "I love thee, O Lord." David sang songs about his love for God. He taught others to sing his songs and write their own songs about their love for God. David demonstrated his love for God through his worship and music. There were times when David disappointed God, to be sure, but he loved Him.

Have you ever wondered why it is that Jesus was called the Son of David? Obviously, he was called that because he was. But, David was only one of the progenitors of Jesus. Jesus isn't called the son of Jeconiah, or Zerubbabel, or Eliakim. He wasn't even called the son of Solomon, Asa, Jehoshaphat, Hezekiah, or Josiah. No, Jesus was called the "son of David." Jesus even referred to Himself as the son of David (Matt. 22:45). Certainly, there were Messianic implications in the association of Jesus was David. But, the bigger question is, "Why David?" The answer is simple. It is because David was a man after God's own heart.

We've learned some very important things about David through this study of his life. We learned that David was sought (1 Sam. 13:14), found (Ps. 89:20; Acts 13:22), chosen (1 Kings 8:16; Ps. 78:70; 89:3), and appointed (1 Sam. 13:14). God was looking for him, found him, and established David in the position for which God had prepared him.

In this study, we have looked at four passages that highlight what God looking for and how He found it in David. We saw from 1 Samuel 13:14 that God was looking for a man with a heart like His. The passage teaches us that our character needs to be like the heart of God for God to take notice.

The second passage that describes God's search is Psalm 89:20. This passage emphasizes the servanthood of David. God found in David a servant. David was willing to be used of God. In fact, the Psalmist records God's exclamation, "I have found David My servant." You can almost hear the excitement in God's voice. We learn from this passage that God is looking for men who will be faithful to serve Him. That means we must be willing to work on His agenda not our own. It means that we must be willing to yield to His will and His time if we want to be a man after His heart.

The third passage describing God's discovery of David is Acts 7:46. This passage describes the vision of David's heart to build for the Lord a Temple. This wasn't just a dream of David's to make himself famous. He longed for a permanent place of worship for the Lord. David's desire pleased God because David was looking beyond himself, his wishes, and even his life-time. David wanted what God wanted. Even when God affirmed David's vision, but not David's part in it, David rejoiced knowing that what he had seen (the Temple) would become a reality and that he would have a part in seeing it accomplished. This passage reminds us of the importance of seeing as God sees. Too often we have such small visions and dreams of what God could do through our lives. Maybe, we need to catch God's vision for our lives? For our churches?

The final passage that portrays what God found in David is Acts 13:22. In this passage, David is contrasted with Saul as God points out that unlike his predecessor, David would do all that God desired. We've clearly seen that David was not a perfect man. In fact, he was far from it. In fact, the Bible records more sins committed by David than any other person. Yet, the Bible declares that he did all of God's will. That doesn't mean he always did God's will. It means he accomplished everything that God wanted him to accomplish. This passage speaks to the ultimate mission of our lives. We've seen that God has big plans for all of our lives. We fit in the perfect master plan that God has been preparing since before time began. The question isn't, "Is God ready to fulfill His purpose in your life?" The question is, "Are you ready to fulfill His purpose in your life?" We must never be satisfied with less than all that God wants to do in and through us.

So, the real question of this journey is "How can you and I become a man after God's own heart?" I'm not content just knowing David was that man. I want to be that man. I want you to be that man. God found in David a man of character, a servant, a man of vision, and a man of mission. It was those attributes that stand out among the many wonderful things about David that most pleased God. If that's so, doesn't it make sense that if you and I want to be men after God's own heart today, that's where we need to begin? After all, God is still looking for a few good men. He's looking for men after His heart. How's your character? Are you demonstrating by who you are and how you live that God has made a difference in your life. Johnny Hunt says, "You cannot make a difference until you're different."[64] You won't be perfect, but you can be more faithful. You won't always get it right, but you can seek Him for direction. You won't always see the bigger picture that God has for your life and His church, but you can trust that God sees what you can't see and will work out His will through your faithful submission.

David was sought, found, chosen, and appointed. But, all of those things could be true of you. God has sought you. He may still be seeking you. He wants to prepare you to be the man that He created you to be. If you will trust Him, He will faithfully complete the task that He has begun in you.

In the end, the words of God to Ezekiel well-fit our time. God said that He "sought for a man among them who would make a wall, and stand in the gap before Me on behalf of the land, that I should not destroy it; but I found no one (Ezek. 22:30)." May it never be true today that God still can't find that man!

Don't try to be a man after God's own heart so people will say that about you. Be a man after God's Heart because that's who God created you to be.

The Marks of a Man After God's Heart

Someone asked me recently, as a result of hearing about my work on this book, "How do you know if you are a man after God's heart?" In other words, "What would that look like?" That's the key question of this book. I want to close by examining the marks of a man after God's heart.

Some preliminary thoughts are in order. First, it is God who makes the determination of a man after God's heart. That doesn't come from you or me, or anyone else. You and I might be able to fool others; we might even be able to fool ourselves. But, we can't fool God. It is significant to note that David didn't call himself a man after God's heart, God did.

If you and I are living our lives according to the standards that we have set for ourselves, or if we are living our lives to please others, we are missing the mark. In David's confession, he reminded us that we are ultimately accountable to God.[65] Jesus asked a very probing question when he asked what difference would it make if a person gained the entire world, but lost his or her soul?[66] Too many people waste too much of their lives living for the applause of the wrong audience. But, if you want to be a man

after God's heart, you have to follow His standards, because God decides who is like Him.

One other preliminary thought about becoming a man after God's heart, it's not an accomplishment, it's a lifelong journey. Becoming a man after God's heart isn't something that you will ever be able to check off your to-do list and then move on to other pursuits. Meeting God's standards today doesn't guarantee that you won't fail them tomorrow. You and I must continually, regularly commit our lives to His standards if we are going to follow His heart.

It is God's determination, and it is a lifelong pursuit but Scripture has given us some clues on how we know we are becoming a man after God's heart. I've called these marks of a man after God's heart.

The first mark of a man after God's heart is a genuine and growing love for the Lord. Despite David's failures, it is clear that his love for the Lord was the driving factor in his life. David proclaimed in Psalm 18:1, "I will love You, O Lord, my strength." David's love for the Lord was seen in his desire for the things of the Lord. David demonstrated his love through his obedience, his gifts to the Lord, and desire to provide a permanent place for the Lord.

If you and I want to be men after God's heart, it requires a love relationship with Him. That's not just obedience, and it's not just good intentions. Moses explained that God expects His people to "love the Lord your God with all your heart, and with all your soul, and with all of your strength."[67] One can't just "sort of" love God. Either you love Him or you do not. God wants your highest affection which begins with the recognition of who He is, leads to obedience, and overflows through us. This is the kind of love that Jesus three times asked Peter if he had for Him. What about you? Do you love Him? You can't be a man of God unless you do.

A second mark of a man after God's own heart is a passionate hunger for God's Word. You don't love God if you don't follow His Word. Jesus said, "If anyone loves Me, he will keep My word."[68] His Word is absolute, unchanging, and non-negotiable. David demonstrated a genuine love of God's Word. We saw this most clearly demonstrated in David through his music. He didn't just talk about God's Word, he studied God's Word; sought God's Word; desired God's Word.

David's words in Psalm 119:9 and 11 seem to foreshadow[69] the answer to the puzzling question of how he could demonstrate such faithfulness and yet commit such heinous sins. In verse nine he rhetorically asked how a young man can keep his way pure and confirms that it is only when he lives according to God's Word. Then, in verse eleven, he promised, "your word I have hidden in my heart that I might not sin against you." In the end, that may be the key to understanding how David could achieve such heights in his relationship with the Lord and yet fail so scandalously. He walked nearest to God when he kept most closely to His Word.

Maybe you've noticed that in your own life. In those times when your walk with the Lord is most genuine, you find you hear God most clearly. Then, when you become negligent in your commitment to God's Word, you feel the most distant from Him. Those are the times when you feel like your prayers are seem void, your worship seems stale, your assurance seems shaky, and your love for Him feels shallow. Ours in probably not the time about which the prophet Amos spoke when he prophesied a famine for hearing the Word of God,[70] and yet there may have been times in your life when it seemed like it was. When you face those moments of barrenness and drought, those are the times when you need God the most. The irony is that so often when we need God most, we seek Him the least. Seek Him through prayer. Seek Him through His Word. God desires to speak to you. His Word is fresh and alive and relevant. A man of God must be a man of God's Word.

A third mark of a man after God's heart is a lifelong pursuit of holiness. I am a student of the spiritual awakenings in the Old Testament. Of the 10 good Kings in Israel's long history,[71] there were several significant spiritual awakenings. The tragedy was that they didn't last very long. While there were a number of reasons for the brevity of these awakenings,[72] the number one reason was carelessness in holiness. Never forget, God has high standards. Moreover, He isn't going to lower His standards just because we fail to reach them. God still demands that we "be holy because I, the Lord your God, am holy."[73] Jesus reiterated those same words in Matthew 5:48, when He said that we are to be perfect even as God is perfect. With those as the standards, it's no wonder that all of us fall short. But that is no excuse to stop trying. Even as the Apostle Paul proclaimed, I'm not there yet, but "I press on."[74] Is that true for you? Are you growing closer to Christ and becoming more and more like Him? John said that when we see Him we will be like Him because we will see Him as He truly is.[75] If that's true, shouldn't it also be true that as we grow in our relationship with Him, spending more time with God's people and in His Word, that we will become more like Him?

David wasn't always like Him, but there were times when He appeared to be very close. His desire was to become more like Him, as expressed in the agony of his repentance and the joy of his forgiveness.[76] There were times when he didn't get it right, but those were the times when he sought to make it right. The Bible declares that no one is sinless,[77] but that doesn't mean that we have to sin. It just means that we do. Don't grow complacent; God has made a way for you to be holy. You don't have to sin. You can be like Him, by living according to the standards of His Word. We've seen the devastating consequences of those who have failed, wouldn't it be something to see what God would do through someone who lived right. If you want to be a man after God's heart, never forget, God's heart is holy.

It won't be good enough to be good for a little while. God doesn't grade on a curve or based on our good intentions. He expects you and me to be on a lifelong pursuit of holiness. That's the mark of a Godly man.

A fourth mark of a man after God's heart is an honest desire for authentic worship. David revolutionized worship. He brought his love of music and passion for God's Word together with his desire to seek the Lord's presence. Worship isn't just about music or drama or even preaching. In fact, worship is not about us at all. Worship is about God. He's the audience; He's the recipient. If you come to God's house for any other reason except to encounter God and honor and praise him with the sacrifice of your life, you're there for the wrong reason.

One of the passions of David's heart was to build a Temple unto the Lord. But it wasn't just so David could brag about what he had done. David wanted a permanent place for the Lord's presence to dwell among His people. A place where the Ark of the Covenant could reside, sacrifices could be made, and the Lord to could be sought. The Temple wasn't for David or Israel, it was for the Lord.

Sadly, too often as men, we have devalued worship. We don't always participate passionately in the singing of our praise to the Lord and we aren't always as faithful in our attendance as we should be. Part of that is because our definition of worship is missing something. Worship has very little to do with what we do. It is all about the One for whom we do it.

David's wife didn't understand it, the people didn't always follow his example, and even David didn't always get it right. But he had a desire to worship the Lord. David passionately expressed the desire of his heart for worship in Psalm 42. In that Psalm he describes his longing for the presence of the Lord and the joy and praise that accompanied his worship. What about you? Do you long to worship God? Do you look forward to spending time with God's people in God's house? If it's missing, plead with God to restore to you (or maybe give to you for the first time) the joy of genuine and transparent worship of the Lord. He is worthy of your worship, and what's more, you need the experience of being in His presence. It's what a man after God's own heart does.

A fifth mark of a man after God's heart is a contagious Kingdom perspective. This is the kind of perspective that realizes that this life isn't just about you and me. We need to see the big picture. Ultimately, your needs, desires, and comfort may not be God's will. Even as Jesus demonstrated in the garden His desire for God's will over His own comfort, you and I must strive to live the "nevertheless" of Jesus' prayer. Do you desire God's will for your life more than you desire your own?

The Marks of a Godly Man

1. *A genuine and growing love of Christ*

2. *A passionate hunger for God's Word*

3. *A lifelong pursuit of holiness*

4. *An honest desire for authentic worship*

5. *A contagious Kingdom perspective*

A man with a contagious Kingdom perspective has an impact on people around him. He can't help it. If your love for the Lord is that real to you, people will know it, they will see it, and they will be impacted by it. A man after God's heart will be concerned with fulfilling our Lord's great commission and taking the Gospel to the entire world. We can't be like God's heart and only be concerned about our needs. We can't just want what we want and strive to satisfy the desire of His heart.

The prophet Zechariah talks about a day when people of all nations will seek the Lord. They will be so eager to find Him that they will do whatever it takes to get to Him. He describes a day when "ten men from every language of the nations shall grasp the sleeve of a Jewish man, saying, 'Let us go with you, for we have heard *that* God *is* with you'" (Zech. 8:23). Would that that would be said of your life and mine. Wouldn't it be great if people said that about our churches?

When your desire for His will to be done exceeds your own, you're on your way to becoming a man after God's heart. That's the kind of man who will make a difference in our communities, in our families, and in our churches. You can be a man after God's heart. You've just got to do it His way! Start today. Start right now. God is watching, the church is waiting, and the world is wondering will you be a man after God's heart.

Appendix One

For the Sake of My Servant David

What God did NOT do "for the sake of [His] servant David . . ."

1. The *whole* kingdom was NOT torn away under Solomon or his successors - 1 Kings 11:12, 13, 32, and 34.
2. God left a lamp in Jerusalem for David's sake under Abijam - 1 Kings 15:3-5
3. The Lord would not destroy Judah under Jehoram because He promised to leave a lamp to David and his sons forever- 2 Kings 8:19
4. God would not give Judah to Assyria under Hezekiah - 2 Kings 19:34; Isaiah 37:35
5. God added 15 years to Hezekiah's life - 2 Kings 20:6

Psalm 132:10 – "For Your servant David's sake, do not turn away the face of Your Anointed."

Appendix Two

DAVID AND THE SINGERS IN CHRONICLES

A. Very little, if any, treatment is given to the role of the singers in the Kings or Samuel

    1. Cf. the bringing of the Ark to Jerusalem in 2 Sam. 6 & 1 Chron. 15 (vs.16, 27-28)
    2. Cf. the Ark brought into the Temple in 1 Kings 8 & 2 Chron. 5 (vs. 12-13)
    3. Cf. the dedication of the Temple in 1 Kings 8:62-66 & 2 Chron. 7:6

B. David's background with music. David was the King; but his background was as a musician

C. David established that the offerings to the Lord were to be made with rejoicing and singing – 2 Chron. 23:18

D. The emphasis on singers in Chronicles is unique – could have implications on dating of the book if the author was giving instructions for the new Temple

E. The Levite Singers - 1 Chron. 6:31-48
- NOTE: Ezra 8:15 – Ezra delayed returning to Jerusalem for 3 days because there were not any Levites returning with him. At least part of their responsibility would have been for music

F. Asaph and his sons , Heman and his sons, Ethan, and the sons Jeduthun

    1. Their Clothing – clothed in robes (1 Chron. 15:27)

    2. Their Calling
- They were set apart (1 Chron. 25:1)
- They served by rotation determined by casting of lots (1 Chron. 25:8-31)

    3. Their Function – They were Prophets - They should **prophesy** with harps, stringed instruments, and cymbals (1 Chron. 25:1- 3)

    4. Their Responsibility
      a. They sang (1 Chron. 6:33; 15:16, 19, 22, 27; 2 Chron. 5:12; 23:18; 29:30)

    b. They were stationed in the Temple (2 Chron. 29:25)

    c. They were free from other service in the Temple (1 Chron. 9:33)

    d. They were engaged in their work night and day (1 Chron. 9:33)

    e. They were heads of households, chief men who lived in Jerusalem (1 Chron. 9:34)

    f. They stood beside the altar as the Ark was brought into the Temple (2 Chron. 5:11-14; Cf. 1 Chron. 16:4)

5. Their Role in sacrifices (2 Chron. 29:30)
   - They sang praises praise to the Lord as offerings were being made

6. Their Role in Battle
   a. Led the people into battle – (1 Chron. 25:1; 2 Chron. 13:12, 14; 20:21-22)
   b. Celebrated victory through music – (2 Chron. 20:28)

7. Their Skill (1 Chron. 15:22; 25:1,7; 2 Chron. 34:12)

8. Their Instruments (1 Chron. 13:8; 15:16, 42; 25:1, 3, 6; 2 Chron. 5:12;

7:6; 29:25-27; 34:12)

9. Their Unison (2 Chron. 5:13)

     a. They sang and played as one

     b. The glory of the Lord accompanied their praise

10. They Led in Praise and Thanksgiving (2 Chron. 5:13; 23:13; 30: 21; 31:2; Cf. 1 Chron. 16:4, 7)

11. Their Role in the Passover and Festivals (2 Chron. 30:21; 35:15)

12. Their Work with the Prophets (2 Chron. 35:25)

G. Psalms of Asaph

    1.   Psalm 50

    2.   Psalms 73-83

NOTE: Ps. 78 – its emphasis on David and his heart

H. Psalm of Heman - Psalm 88

I. Psalm of Ethan - Psalm 89
    NOTE: The emphasis of this Psalm on David as God's servant

J. Psalms Dedicated to Jeduthun - Psalm 39, 62, 77

End Notes

1   McCarter, "The Historical David," 117.

2   See R. T. Kendall, *A Man After God's Own Heart* (Geanies House, Fearn, Ross-shire, Great Britain: Christian Focus Publications, 2001), 13. Kendall points out that God took the initiative in seeking out a man.

3   See John Goldingay, *Psalms: Volume 1: Psalms 1-41, Baker Commentary on the Old Testament Wisdom and Psalms*, ed. Tremper Longman III. (Grand Rapids: Baker Academic, 2006): 26-30. Goldingay discusses the various alternatives that have been proffered with reference to the phrase, "of David."

4   The Psalms of David include: Psalms 3-9; 11-32; 34-41; 51-65; 68-70; 86; 101; 103; 108-110; 122; 124; 131; 133; 138-145; and 2 Sam. 23:1-7. Note that 2 Sam. 22:1-51 contains David's Psalm celebrating the Lord's deliverance for him from Saul. This Psalm is virtually identical to Psalm 18. Also, 1 Chron. 16:8-36 contains elements of at least 3 other Psalms which may or may not have been Davidic: Ps. 105:1-15; 96:1-13; 106:1, 47-48 serve as the sources for 1 Chron. 16:8-22; 23-33, 34, 35-36 respectively.

5   The Dead Sea Scrolls manuscript 11QPsa indicated that David actually wrote 4050 psalms. Additionally, a discovery near Jericho included more than 200 Psalms supposedly attributed to David that are not included in the Bible.

6   Stephen Olford, in the forward to Gene Getz, *David: Seeking God Faithfully* Nashville: Broadman and Holman, 1995), ix.

7   Kendall, 97. David's sin almost cost Jonathan his life when his father attempted to kill him with his spear because Saul knew that Jonathan was covering for David.

8   See Robert B. Chishom, Jr. "Cracks in the Foundation: Ominous Sings in the David Narrative" (paper presented at the national meeting of the Evangelical Theological Society, Providence, Rhode Island, 19 November 2008), 13. Chisholm contends that David "was unable to deal justly with those closest to him."

9   See Jerry Vines, *Pursuing God's Own Heart* (Nashville: Broadman and Holman, 2003), 209. Vines described how David tried to use Uriah to cover up his sin with Bathsheba. He even got Uriah drunk, but this faithful servant would not consent to the comforts of home when his fellow soldiers were in battle for the Lord. Vines pointed out that Uriah was a better man drunk than David was sober.

10 Cf. the period of Bathsheba's pregnancy (around 9 months) and 2 Samuel 24:8 which describes a period of nine months and twenty days.

11 See Ralph W. Klein, *1 Samuel,* Word Biblical Commentary, vol. 10 (Waco: TX: Word Books, 1983), 124-25;

Robert D. Bergen, *1, 2 Samuel*, The New American Commentary, vol. 7 (Nashville: Broadman & Holman, 1996), 147-48; P. Kyle McCarter, *1 Samuel,* The Anchor Bible, vol. 8 (Garden City, NY: Doubleday and Co., 1980), 222-23. The Hebrew of this verse is complicated and scholars are not in agreement as to whether the time reference is corrupt, it is referencing Saul's age when he came to the throne, or is suggesting how long Saul had reigned before the events of 13:1 occurred.

12 See Klein, 124-25. Some translations state that Saul was 30 years old when he began to reign, while other stipulate that he was 40 years old. The LXX omits this reference to Saul's age.

13 Cf. Acts 13:21.

14 See F. B. Meyer, *David: Shepherd Psalmist-King* (Grand Rapids: Zondervan Publishing House, 1953), 11.

15 Jack Graham, *A Man of God* (Wheaton, IL: Crossway Books, 2005), 24.

16 Tony W. Cartledge, *I & II Samuel*, Smyth and Helwys Bible Commentary (Macon, GA: Smyth & Helwys, 2001), 175; Robert P. Gordon, *1 & 2 Samuel: A Commentary* (Great Britain: The Paternoster Press, 1986), 134; McCarter, 229. McCarter sees a parallel between "a man of his choice" and the Akkadian expression used at the installation of Nebuchadnezzar, which can be translated "a king of his own choice."

17 Chisholm, 1; Julius Wellhausen *Prolegomena to the History of Ancient Israel*, trans. Allan Menzies and J. Sutherland Black (Cleveland: Meridian Books, 1957), 182; Jacob Myers, *1 Chronicles,* in vol. 12 of *The Anchor Bible*, xviii,

xxx, lxiii.; and P. Kyle McCarter, Jr., "The Historical David," *Interpretation*, 40, no. 2, (April 1986), 117-19. See also Mark A. Throntveit, "Was the Chronicler a Spin Doctor? David in the Books of Chronicles," *Word & World* 23 (Fall 2003): 374-81. Throntveit rightly concludes that the Chronicler includes David's faults as well as his faith. He points out that the significance of the treatment of David in Chronicles has more to do with the particular needs of the audience the Chronicler was addressing and the purpose of his work.

18 Jeffrey L. Townsend, "The Purpose of 1 and 2 Chronicles," *Bibliotheca Sacra* (July-September 1987), 291.

19 See The Barna Group, March 6, 2000, "Women Are the Backbone of the Christian Congregations in America," from http://www.barna.org/FlexPage.aspx?Page=BarnaUpdate&BarnaUpdateID=47; Hartford Institute for Religion Research, "Men's Commitment to Religion: Perceptions of its Nature, Nurture, and Consequences," from http://hirr.hartsem.edu/bookshelf/lummis_article2.html; The United Methodist Church, "Report of the Men's Study of the United Methodist Church Approved by the 2004 General Conference," from http://www.gcumm.org/atf/cf/%7BD9A427F4-2689-4788-A16C-9CEC60F33E7F%7D/MM%20Study%202008.pdf; New Man Magazine, "Men Unchallenged by Church," from http://www.newmanmag.com/display.php?id=9296&print=yes; LifeSiteNews, "Dying Church of England Now Ordaining More Women Than Men," from http://www.lifesitenews.com/ldn/2007/nov/07111502.html; The Christian Index, "Book Tells What Women Wish Pastors Knew," from http://www.christianindex.org/3026.article; United States Conference on Catholic Bishops, "Sociological and

Cultural Issues Affecting the Rise of Priestly Vocations in North America," from http://www.usccb.org/vocations/articles/seminarium.shtml.

20 The Barna Group, March 6, 2000, "Women Are the Backbone of the Christian Congregations in America," from: http://www.barna.org/FlexPage.aspx?Page=BarnaUpdate&BarnaUpdateID=47.

21 See Kendall, 35. Kendall points out that while "David had the anointing, Saul [still] had the crown."

22 Henry Blackaby, *The Man God Uses* (Nashville: Broadman and Holman, 1999), 169.

23 Mike Bickle, *After God's Heart: The Key to Knowing and Living God's Passionate Love for You* (Lake Mary, FL: Charisma House, 2009), 161-62.

24 Cf. 1 Sam. 13:14; Ps. 89:20; Acts 7:46; 13:22. These passages will become the focus of the remaining chapters.

25 Isaiah 55:10-11.

26 See Tamara C. Eskenazi, "A Literary Approach to Chronicles' Ark Narrative in 1 Chronicles 13-16," in *Fortunate the Eyes that See: Essays in Honor of David Noel Freedman in Celebration of His Seventieth Birthday*, ed. Astrid B. Beck, Andrew H. Bartelt, Paul R. Raabe, and Chris A. Franke (Grand Rapids: William B. Eerdmans Publishing Co., 1995), 265-66. Eskenazi also notes that interesting change of language with reference to the ark after the Levites faithfully transported it. Previously, it was common to refer to the ark as the ark of God. After the Levites carried the ark according to the parameters

in Scripture and brought it to the place that David established for it, it was frequently referred to as the Ark of the Covenant. She suggests that the language implies that the Covenant became effective upon their obedience to faithfully follows Gods guidelines. Thus, the covenant would be emphasized as conditioned on mankind's obedience to its stipulations.

27 Ibid., 265. Eskenazi points out the contrast between David's heart and Saul's heart in the language of the Hebrew text. She points out the repetition of the words, "turn" and "seek" in 1 Chron. 10:14 and 13:3. In 13:3, David urges the people to "turn" the ark of God to them recognizing that during Saul's reign, they did not "seek" the Lord. While in 10:14, we saw that because Saul did not "seek" the Lord, the kingdom would be "turned" over to David.

28 See H. Edwin Young, *David: After God's Own Heart* (Nashville: Broadman Press, 1984), 16.

29 Words and music to "Ruin Me" are by Jeff Johnson.

30 Mark J. Boda, *After God's Own Heart: The Gospel According to David* (Phillipsburg, NJ: P & R Publishing Co., 2007), 103.

31 2 Samuel 3:18; 7:5, 8; 1 Kings 11:13, 32, 34, 36, 38; 14:8; 19:34; 20:6; 1 Chronicles 17:4, 7; Psalm 89:3, 20; Isaiah 37:35; Jeremiah 33:21, 22, 26; Ezekiel 34:23, 24, 25.

32 Vines, 20. Vines points out that while everyone else noticed that David was smaller than Goliath, David, more importantly, recognized that Goliath was smaller than God.

33 Deut. 7:6; 14:2; Isa. 41:8, 9; 43:10; 44:2; 45:4; 49:7; Amos 3:2; Luke 12:32; John 13:18; 2 Thes. 2:13; 1 Peter 2:9.

34 Waylon B. Moore, *The Power of a Mentor* (Tampa, FL: Missions Unlimited, Inc., 1996), 13.

35 Waylon Moore, *Mentoring*, vol. 26, no. 1, May 2007, 2.

36 It is used of Abigail in 1 Samuel 25:3, whom David later marries because she demonstrates wisdom; David in 2 Chronicles 2:12; Hezekiah in 2 Kings 18:7 and 2 Chronicles 30:22; and Sherebiah in Ezra 8:18, who served with Ezra in teaching the people the law.

37 Cf. 1 Chron. 12:19. This passage indicates that while David was fleeing from Saul, some of Saul's people from Manasseh defected to David. David was beginning to have an impact on all of Israel.

38 See Robert B. Chisholm, Jr. *Interpreting the Historical Books: An Exegetical* Handbook (Grand Rapids: Kregel Publications, 2006), 175-77. The Hebrew text here is complicated and several options have been put forth as to the actual identity and name of the giant that Elhanan killed. Chisholm concludes that every option that has been presented is problematic. See also J. A. Thompson, *1, 2 Chronicles,* New American Commentary, vol. 9 (Nashville: Broadman and Holman: 1994): 157-58.

39 Compare 1 Kings 14:22-24, which stipulates his sin as idolatry.

40 Thompson, 266. The nine references are 14:4, 7 (twice);

15:2, 4, 12, 13, 15; 16:12.

41 See Deut. 26:5.

42 Bickle, 153.

43 Ibid., 153-55.

44 Rick Warren, *Purpose-Driven Church* (Grand Rapids: Zondervan, 1995), 87.

45 See Appendix II for a discussion of David and the Singers in Chronicles.

46 Some have objected that the name Baal can also mean "lord." However, while that this is so is even more indication of the syncretism of Saul's faith. He wanted to worship God his own way and if that meant applying some of the elements of the Canaanite religion, that was ok. A person of genuine faith would be repulsed to have the name of a pagan god as part of their name. However, it seems to have been a part of at least 3 consecutive generations of Saul's family.

47 Of the twenty-one kings who reigned after David, ten of them were compared either positively or negatively to David. In 1 Kings 11:4, 6, 33-34, 38, Solomon was extolled for being good, but not like David; 2 Chron. 11:17 says that for three years Rehoboam did well because he walked in the ways of David; 1 Kings 15:3 says that Abijah was good, but not like David; 1 Kings 15:11 says that Asa did right like his father David; 2 Chron. 17:3 says that Jehoshaphat did right in the eyes of the Lord like his father David; 2 Chron. 21:6-7 says that Jehoram walked in the ways of the kings of Israel, but God would not destroy his house on account of

David; 2 Kings 14:3 says that Amaziah was good, but
not like David; 2 Kings 16:2 says that Ahaz did not do
like his father David; 2 Chron. 29:2 says that Hezekiah
did right like his father David; and 2 Chron. 34:2 says
that Josiah did what was right before the Lord like his
father David had done.

48 See Vines, 236-38; John Philips, *Exploring Proverbs: An
Expository Commentary*, vol. 2 (Grand Rapids: Kregel,
2002): 98-99; Martha A. Crawford, *Don't Give Up!
Keep Going* (Palo Alto, CA: Fultus Corporation, 2005),
71-72. Cf. Robert D. Bergen, *1,2 Samuel*, The New
American Commentary, vol. 7 (Nashville: Broadman
and Holman, 1996): 432. Bergen suggests that Barzillai
did not find the king's offer appealing. Bergen suggested
that Barzillai felt like he would no longer be the most
important person in his community if we went with
King David.

49 See Eugene Peterson, *First and Second Samuel* (Louisville:
Westminster John Knox Press, 1999), 233. Peterson
suggests that Barzillai wants nothing from David and
needs nothing from him. He is simply a man with a pure
motive escorting the king across the Jordan (1 Sam.
19:31).

50 Some Greek manuscripts, like the Septuagint, suggest
that Chimham may have been the son of Barzillai.

51 Cf. 1 Sam. 17:27-29.

52 F. B. Huey, *Jeremiah Lamentations*, The New American
Commentary, vol. 16 (Nashville: Broadman Press,
1993): 356.

53 Vines, 239; Edgar Whitaker Work, *The House of Chimham*

(American Tract Society, 1909), 39-40. Whitaker also suggests that the land David gave to Chimham also encompassed the land where he formerly shepherded his sheep as a youth.

54 Kendall, 12.

55 Theodore H. Epp, *A Man After the Heart of God* (Lincoln, NE: Back to the Bible Broadcast, 1965), 201.

56 See Psalms 9, 22, 24, 57, 60, 86, 108, and 145.

57 Vines, 161.

58 1 Pet. 4:10.

59 Taken from "Real Last Words of Famous People," http://www.mapping.com/words.html on June 29, 2009.

60 See Thompson, 127.

61 See Jim George, *A Man After God's Own Heart: Devoting Your Life to What Really Matters* (Eugene, OR: Harvest House Publishers, 2008), 45. George affirms that the marks of Godly men in the Bible are the same marks that need to be evident in the lives of men today.

62 See above note 31.

63 See Luis Palau. *Heart After God: Running With David* (Portland, OR: Multnomah Press, 1978), 35.

64 Johnny M. Hunt, *Building Your Spiritual Resume: Developing a Testimony that will outlast you* (Woodstock, GA: 3H Publishers, 200), 98.

65 See Psalm 51.

66 Matt. 16:26.

67 Deut. 6:5.

68 John 14:23.

69 When was Psalm 119 written?

70 Amos 8:11.

71 During the divided kingdom, Israel had twenty kings, none of them were described as good. After the division, Judah also had twenty monarchs, of which, eight were labeled good. Counting David and Solomon, that makes ten kings who earned the label of good out of a total of forty-two kings between the two kingdoms.

72 See my study of "Why Lasting Revivals are Rare."

73 Lev. 19:1.

74 Phil. 3:14.

75 1 John 3:2.

76 See Psalms 32 and 51.

77 See Romans 3:23. See also Gen. 6:9, Job 1:1; and Dan. 1;4, 8; 6:4. In these three passages, Noah, Job, and Daniel are described as perfect. Interestingly, the Lord seems to refer to that in Ezek. 14:14, and 20 when He declared that even if Noah, Job, and Daniel were to intercede for Judah, He would not pardon it of its sin. However, the Lord added that they would be able

to rescue themselves because of their righteousness. Evidently, though the Bible says that no one is perfect, and we know of some failures on the part of Noah and Job, there were periods in these men's lives in which they were.

LaVergne, TN USA
11 October 2009
160500LV00002B/2/P